Blest Are We®
Faith in Action

Thus faith comes from what is heard,
and what is heard comes through the word of Christ.

Romans 10:17

Charley Cook
Corporate Vice President
Kendall Hunt Publishing

Anne P. Battes
Publisher

Mary Sellars Malloy
Project Manager

Mary Wessel
Graphic Designer

GRADE ONE
PARISH EDITION

RCL Benziger®

a Kendall Hunt Company
Cincinnati, Ohio

"The Subcommittee on the Catechism, United States Conference of Catholic Bishops, has found this catechetical series, copyright 2019 to be in conformity with the *Catechism of the Catholic Church*."

Nihil Obstat Imprimatur

✝ Most Reverend Joseph R. Binzer
Auxiliary Bishop
Vicar General
Archdiocese of Cincinnati
February 21, 2018

The *nihil obstat* and *imprimatur* are official declarations that a book or pamphlet is free of doctrinal and moral error. No implication is contained therein that those who have granted the *nihil obstat* and *imprimatur* agree with the contents, opinions, or statements expressed.

Blest Are We Faith in Action Team

Contributing Writers
Christina De Camp, Kate Sweeney Ristow, Gloria Shahin, Susan Stark
Resources: Marilyn Miller
Revelation: Scripture and Tradition: Rev. Robert J. Hater, PhD
Special Needs: Ann Sherzer
Take Home: Donna N. Glaser
Feasts and Seasons: Ronald C. Lamping, Jo Rotunno

Theological Consultant
Rev. Robert J. Hater, PhD

Editorial Staff
Karen Cain, Project Editor
Elizabeth Shepard, Project Editor
James Spurgin, Editorial Manager
Jo Rotunno, Publisher Emerita

Production Staff
Lori Gray, Graphic Designer
Bob Ishee, Production Manager

Blest Are We Faith & Word Team

Series Authors
Rev. Richard N. Fragomeni, Ph.D.; Maureen Gallagher, Ph.D.; Jeannine Goggin, M.P.S.; Michael P. Horan, Ph.D.

Scripture Co-editor and Consultant
Maria Pascuzzi, S.S.L., S.T.D.

Multicultural Consultant
Angela Erevia, M.C.D.P., M.R.E.

Contributing Writers
Janie Gustafson, Ph.D.
Family Time Scripture: Michael J. Williams, M.S.
Feasts and Seasons: Marianne K. Lenihan
Our Catholic Heritage: Pat Enright

Advisory Board
William C. Allegri, M.A.; Patricia M. Feeley, S.S.J., M.A.; Edmund F. Gordon; Patricia A. Hoffmann; Cris V. Villapando, D.Min.

Consultants
Margaret J. Borders, M.R.S.; Kelly O'Lague Dulka, M.S.W.; Diane Hardick, M.A.; Debra Schurko; Linda S. Tonelli, M.Ed.; Joy Vilotti-Biedrzycki

Music Advisors
GIA Publications: Michael A. Cymbala, Alec Harris, Robert W. Piercy

Acknowledgments
Excerpts from the English translation of the *Roman Missal* © 2010, ICEL. All rights reserved.

Excerpts from *Catholic Household Blessings and Prayers* (revised edition) © 2007, United States Conference of Catholic Bishops, Washington, D.C.

Excerpts from *The New American Bible, Revised Edition* © 2010, 1991, 1986, 1970 Confraternity of Christian Doctrine, Inc., Washington, D.C. Used with permission. All rights reserved. All adaptations of Scripture are based on the *New American Bible, Revised Edition*.

Textbook only:	444442	ISBN: 978-1-5249-4442-1
Textbook with eBook:	444436	ISBN: 978-1-5249-4436-0

1st Printing
March 2018

Contents

Unit 2 Our Loving God **65**

Unit 5

Jesus' Church of Followers **191**

Unit Song • "Laudate Dominum" 192

Feasts and Seasons

Our Catholic Heritage

Organized according to the four pillars of the Catechism

Let Us Pray

GO TO BlestAreWe.com for Latin texts, Latin pronunciation guides, and Spanish texts for the Sign of the Cross, the Lord's Prayer, the Hail Mary, and the Glory Be.

The Sign of the Cross

In the name of the Father,
and of the Son,
and of the Holy Spirit.
Amen.

Signum Crucis

In nómine Patris,
et Fílii,
et Spíritus Sancti.
Amen.

Señal de la Cruz

En el nombre del Padre,
y del Hijo,
y del Espíritu Santo.
Amén.

The Lord's Prayer

Our Father, who art in heaven,
hallowed be thy name;
thy kingdom come,
thy will be done
on earth as it is in heaven.
Give us this day our daily bread,
and forgive us our trespasses,
as we forgive those who
    trespass against us;
and lead us not into temptation,
but deliver us from evil.
Amen.

The Hail Mary

Hail, Mary, full of grace,
the Lord is with thee.
Blessed art thou among women
and blessed is the fruit of thy
    womb, Jesus.
Holy Mary, Mother of God,
pray for us sinners,
now and at the hour of our death.
Amen.

Glory Be

Glory be to the Father
and to the Son
and to the Holy Spirit,
as it was in the beginning
is now, and ever shall be
world without end.
Amen.

Angel of God

Angel of God,
my guardian dear,
to whom God's love commits
   me here,
ever this day be at my side,
to light and guard, to rule
   and guide.
Amen.

Grace Before Meals

Bless us, O Lord,
and these thy gifts,
which we are about to
receive from thy bounty,
through Christ our Lord.
Amen.

Grace After Meals

We give thee thanks,
for all thy benefits,
almighty God,
who lives and
reigns forever.
Amen.

Morning Prayer

Loving God, bless the work we do.
Watch over us and guide us
in school and at home.
Help us realize that everything
we do gives praise to you.
We make this prayer in Jesus' name.
Amen.

Evening Prayer

Parent: May God bless us and keep us.

Child: **May he guide us in life.**

Parent: May he bless us this evening.

Child: **And keep us in his sight.**

Parent: May God be with you, (name).

Child: **May God be with you, (name).**

Together: In the name of the Father,
and of the Son,
and of the Holy Spirit.
Amen.

My Prayer

_____

- -

_____

- -

_____

- -

_____

- -

_____

- -

_____

- -

_____

Amen.

The Bible

Make known to me your ways, LORD;
teach me your paths. Psalm 25:4

The Bible

The Bible is a special book about God. It has two parts called the Old Testament and the New Testament.

The stories in the Old Testament tell about God's love for his people before Jesus was born.

The New Testament

The stories in the New Testament tell about the life of Jesus and his teachings.

You will learn more about the Bible in Chapter 3.

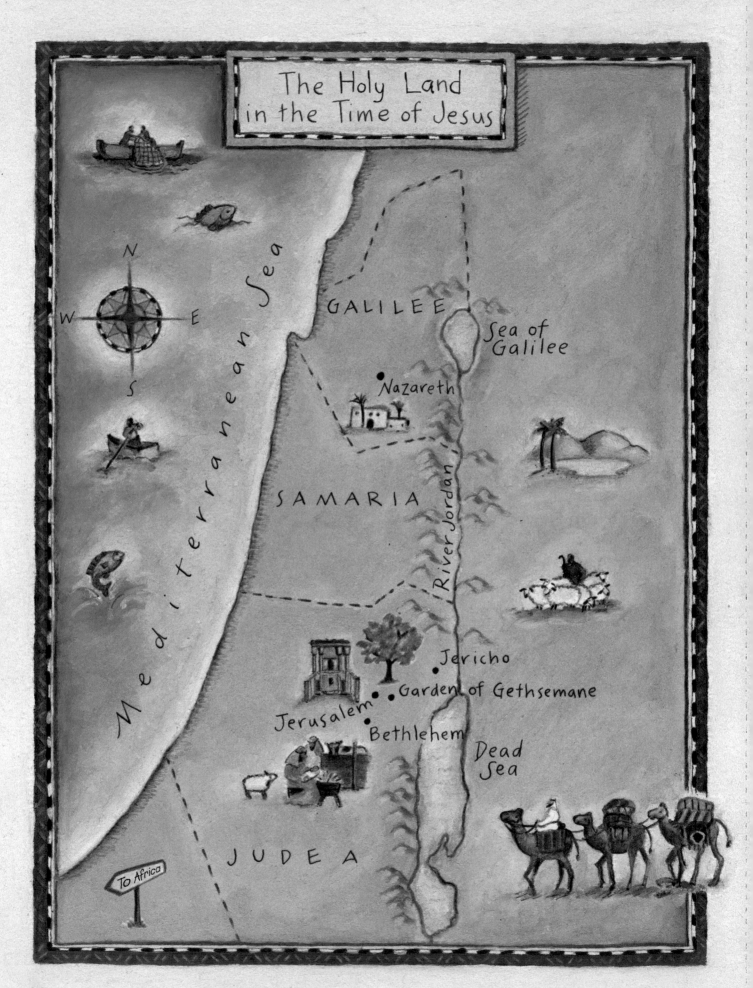

The Holy Land
in the Time of Jesus

N
W   E
S

Mediterranean Sea

GALILEE

Sea of Galilee

Nazareth

SAMARIA

River Jordan

Jerusalem

Jericho

Garden of Gethsemane

Bethlehem

Dead Sea

JUDEA

To Africa

The Map of the Holy Land

The Holy Land map shows places in the time of Jesus. It shows where he lived and worked. It shows where Jesus told people about God's love. You can read about these places in the Bible.

ACTIVITY

Remembering Bible Stories

Look at the pictures from the map. Circle each picture that reminds you of a Bible story. Tell about one of the stories you know.

1.

2.

3.

4.

5.

6.

Blest Are We

Words and Music by David Haas
Spanish translation by Ronald F. Krisman

REFRAIN

Blest are we, ho-ly chil-dren of light__ are__ we!__
¡Ben-de-ci-dos, so-mos san-tos hi-jos de la luz!__

Blest are we, cho-sen peo-ple of God!__
¡Ben-de-ci-dos y e-le-gi-dos por Dios!__

Blest are we, God has plans__ for you and me!__
¡Ben-de-ci-dos, Dios nos quie-re ser cual Je-sús!__

Blest__ are we!__ We are the chil-dren of God!__
¡Ben-de-ci-dos, so-mos los hi-jos de Dios!__

Fine

VERSE

1. For our world,__ each sis-ter and broth-er:
1. Por el mun-do, por to-dos sus pue-blos:

We__ are called,__ called__ to serve!__
¡So-mos lla-ma-dos pa-ra ser-vir!__

We are here to love__ one an-oth-er:
Nos a-me-mos los u-nos a los o-tros;__

We__ are called,__ called__ to serve!__
¡So-mos lla-ma-dos pa-ra ser-vir!__

D.C.

2. For the poor, the meek and the lowly:
   We are called, called to serve!
   For the weak, the sick and the hungry:
   We are called, called to serve!

3. For all those who yearn for freedom:
   We are called, called to serve!
   For the world, to be God's kingdom:
   We are called, called to serve!

2. Por los pobres, los mansos y humildes:
   ¡Somos llamados para servir!
   Por los enfermos, hambrientos, y débiles:
   ¡Somos llamados para servir!

3. Por los que sufren y quieren ser librados:
   ¡Somos llamados para servir!
   Venga a nosotros el Reino de los Cielos:
   ¡Somos llamados para servir!

Our Church Community

With our families, we belong to our Church community. We come together to thank and praise God. We care for one another's needs.

"I am the good shepherd, and I know mine and mine know me, ..."

John 10:14

Jesus cares for each of us just as the shepherd in the picture cares for his sheep. We follow Jesus when we care for people in our Church community.

We Praise You

Words by Mike Balhoff

Music by Darryl Ducote and Gary Daigle

REFRAIN

We praise you, O Lord, for all your works are won-der-ful.

We praise you, O Lord, for ev - er is your love.

VERSE

1. Your wisdom made the heavens and the earth, O Lord;
   You formed the land then set the lights;
   And like your love the sun will rule the day,
   And stars will grace the night.

Text: Mike Balhoff
Tune: Darryl Ducote, Gary Daigle
© 1978, Damean Music. Distributed by GIA Publications, Inc.

Take Home

We Belong to Jesus' Church

In this first chapter your child will learn that your family belongs to the community of Jesus' followers called the Catholic Church. From the Bible story of the Good Shepherd, your child will discover that Jesus calls us each by name to follow him. Finally, your child will learn to pray the Sign of the Cross as a sign of being Catholic.

ACTIVITY Draw a Family Tree

To help your child think about your extended family, draw a family tree and label the branches with the names of relatives you know, both living and deceased.

THROUGH THE WEEK

✝ **A PRAYER FOR THE WEEK** Loving God, bless our family as we begin this day. Help us follow the example of Saint Rose of Lima by loving and caring for others. Amen.

ON SUNDAY

Notice that the Mass begins with the Sign of the Cross. It is a sign that we share as Catholics, no matter what language we speak.

📺 **ON THE WEB**
BlestAreWe.com
RCLBLectionary.com
SaintsResource.com

Saint Rose of Lima (1586–1617)

Rose grew up in a poor family in Lima, Peru. She learned about her faith by listening at Mass. Rose spent long hours in prayer. To serve others, she set up a room in her family's home where poor children and the elderly received free health care. She became the first saint of the Americas.

Feast Day:
August 30

Take Home

 ### Scripture Background
In the Time of Jesus

Shepherds In Palestine a shepherd often walked miles to guide his flock to grass and water. He protected the sheep against attack from predators, often risking his own life. Each evening the shepherd led the flock back to the pen, counting to be sure that no sheep were lost. He knew each sheep, and the sheep responded only to his voice. If even one were missing, the shepherd would go out and try to find it.

You can read Jesus' discourse about the Good Shepherd in John 10:1–21.

Our Catholic Tradition **in Art**

Irish High Crosses During the Viking invasions of Ireland in the eighth and ninth centuries, the Irish erected tall stone crosses throughout the countryside to remind the people of their Christian faith. These High Crosses, decorated with ornamental Celtic art, often contained carvings depicting events from Scripture. The Cross of Muiredach, pictured at left, honors Christ the King, Lord of the Earth. It still stands in County Louth, Ireland.

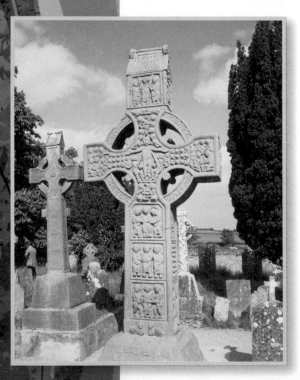

We Belong to Jesus' Church

> **. . . I have called you by name:
> you are mine.** Isaiah 43:1

Share

Everyone belongs to a family.

Families like doing things together.

Look at the picture. What are the families doing?

ACTIVITY

Draw your family at the picnic.

Whom else do you belong to?

The Good Shepherd

Shepherds take care of sheep. A good shepherd knows each sheep by name. The sheep come when they hear the shepherd's voice.

One day Jesus said to his friends, "I am the Good Shepherd. I know you by name. I care for you. You belong to me."

Based on John 10:2–14

We Follow Jesus

Jesus is like a good shepherd. We are like the sheep. Jesus calls us by name. He loves us and cares for us. We follow Jesus.

Our Church Teaches

The **Catholic Church** is a community. A **community** is a group of people who belong together. Our Church community is made up of people who follow Jesus. We love and care for others. We are called Catholics.

ACTIVITY

Write your first name on the sheep. Jesus calls you by name.

What are some things followers of Jesus do?

One Sunday Morning

One Sunday morning Sam and his parents went to a new Catholic church. Some people smiled at them. Some said, "Hi."

"Why did they smile at us?" Sam asked. "Why did they say 'Hi'?"

Sam's mother said, "We are all followers of Jesus. Our Church is like a big family. We care about each other."

Soon Sam had a smile on his face.

Why do you think Sam began to smile?

Tell how these people follow Jesus.
Draw a line from each picture to its word.

help   care   listen   pray

In what ways can
we show that we
are Catholic?

The Sign of the Cross

We use a special sign to show that we belong to the Catholic Church. Say the words and use your right hand to make the Sign of the Cross.

In the name of the Father,

and of the Son,

and of the Holy

Spirit.

Amen.

Chapter Review

A **Circle** the word that best completes each sentence.

1. Jesus said, "I am the _____ Shepherd."

    Lost   **Good**

2. Jesus wants us to _____ others.

    love   **hurt**

3. People who belong to the Catholic Church follow _____ .

    sheep   **Jesus**

4. We make the Sign of the Cross to show that we belong to the _____ Church.

    Catholic   **good**

B **Draw** one way you can follow Jesus.

Faith in Action

Caring and Sharing Our Lady of Mercy School has a Caring and Sharing group. The children and their families help sick and hungry people in the parish. They pray for and visit the sick. They collect and sort food for the hungry.

In Your Parish

ACTIVITY

Draw a line from the car to the house of a friend who is sick. Look at the pictures along the way. Tell ways that people can help.

START

STOP

In Everyday Life

ACTIVITY Think of someone you know who needs help. Think of one thing you can do to help that person. Create a coupon that tells what you are going to do to help him or her.

COUPON

Good for a dog walk

Take Home

We Gather to Celebrate Mass

In this chapter your child will learn that the church building is the place where the parish community gathers to celebrate Mass. Your child will learn that Jesus is present when members of your parish pray together. Some of the sacred objects found in church will also be presented.

ACTIVITY "Here's the Church . . ."

Do you know the fingerplay "Here's the church, here's the steeple, open the doors and see all the people?" If not, the illustrations may help you teach this fingerplay to your child.

THROUGH THE WEEK

✝ **A PRAYER FOR THE WEEK** Lord God, we thank you for calling Saint John Neumann to build up the Church in America. Help us remember that when we gather to pray in our parish church, Jesus is with us. Amen.

ON SUNDAY

Arrive at church early. Notice how the church is decorated and what colors are used for the liturgical season. See what is put on the altar during the celebration of Mass.

🖥 **ON THE WEB**
BlestAreWe.com
RCLBLectionary.com
SaintsResource.com

Saint John Neumann (1811–1860)

John Neumann, born in Bohemia, came to America and became a priest. He was first sent to strengthen the faith of German immigrants near Buffalo, New York. He later became a Redemptorist priest, and before long was ordained a bishop to serve in Philadelphia. While there, 98 Catholic schools and 80 new churches were built.

Feast Day: January 5

Take Home

⚜ Scripture Background
In the Time of Jesus and in the Early Church

The Sign of the Cross Jesus commissioned his disciples with the words of the Sign of the Cross in Matthew 28:16–20. The gestures of the Sign of the Cross can be traced back to the second century, when Christians traced a small cross on their foreheads with their right thumb or a single finger. Two centuries later the large gesture was introduced, using two fingers representing the two natures of Christ. By the end of the Middle Ages, the present form with open hand was common in the West.

Our Catholic Tradition **in Art**

Stained Glass Windows In the Middle Ages illiterate Christians learned Bible stories and stories about saints from stained glass windows. Scenes depicting events from the lives of Christ and the saints were rendered in beautifully colored glass.

The stained glass window at the left is in the Cathedral of Notre Dame in Chartres, France. Forty-two panels tell the story of Noah and the ark. Over one million visitors a year view the windows of the Chartres Cathedral. They are among the world's best preserved records of medieval life.

We Gather to Celebrate Mass

> "For where two or three are gathered together in my name, there am I in the midst of them."
>
> Matthew 18:20

Share

Catholics gather together in church.

Look at these churches.

How are they alike?

How are they different?

ACTIVITY

Draw a picture of your church. How is it like the other two churches on this page? How is it different?

Why do we go to church?

We Gather Together

Each week our Catholic community gathers in **church**. We gather to celebrate **Mass**. Everyone sings a gathering song. Then the priest and the people pray these prayers.

Priest: In the name of the Father, and of the Son, and of the Holy Spirit.

People: **Amen.**

Priest: Grace to you and peace from God our Father and the Lord Jesus Christ.

People: **And with your spirit.**

Roman Missal

The Greeting

The greeting at Mass begins with the Sign of the Cross. The priest says the words. We make the Sign of the Cross with our right hands. Then we say "Amen." At the end of the greeting, the priest asks God to be with us. We ask God to be with the priest.

Our Church Teaches

Our Catholic community is called a **parish**. Jesus is with us when we gather in our parish church. He is with us when we pray. He is with us when our parish community gathers at Mass.

ACTIVITY Sometimes the people say the words below. Trace the letters. Then say the words.

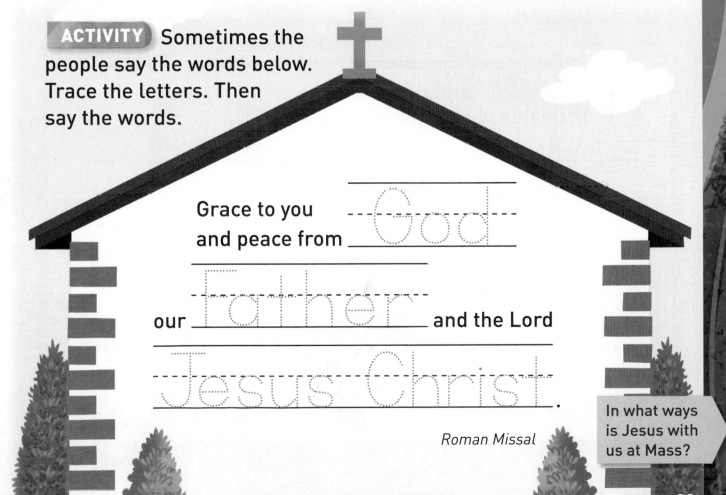

Grace to you and peace from God our Father and the Lord Jesus Christ.

Roman Missal

In what ways is Jesus with us at Mass?

Maria's Parish

Every Sunday Maria and her family go to church. They belong to Saint Anne's Parish. Maria likes to sing and pray with her parish community. She likes to hear about ways her parish helps people. Maria is happy to belong to Saint Anne's Parish.

What do you like about your parish?

ACTIVITY

Write the name of your parish.

_____

_____

_____

_____

Inside a Catholic Church

Parish churches look different on the outside. But they have many things the same on the inside. Some things help us pray. Some are used to celebrate Mass. Here are some of the things in Maria's church.

baptismal font   altar   ambo   crucifix

ACTIVITY

Draw something else that is in your church.

What is one way we can pray?

A Blessing Prayer

God gives us many gifts. We call God's gifts blessings. A **blessing** can also be a prayer. Some blessing prayers ask for God's loving care. Others bless God. Let us pray this prayer to bless God.

Leader: For our parish community,

All: **Blessed be God.**

Leader: For our families and friends,

All: **Blessed be God.**

Leader: For the gift of Jesus,

All: **Blessed be God.**

Child: For (*name a gift from God*),

All: **Blessed be God.**

A **Circle** the word that best completes each sentence.

1. A group of Catholics who belong to the same Church community is called a _____ .

   (parish)   school

2. Catholics gather to celebrate Mass in a _____ .

   (store)   (church)

3. When we gather to pray, _____ is with us.

   everyone   (Jesus)

4. A _____ prayer asks for God's loving care.

   (blessing)   thank you

B **Draw a line** to match each word with its picture.

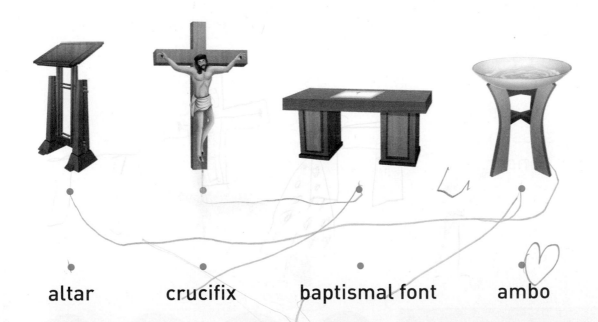

altar   crucifix   baptismal font   ambo

Faith in Action

Church Decorating Many parishes have a group of people who decorate the church. In Advent they set up an Advent wreath. For Easter they use spring flowers and make joyful banners. The group makes the church look beautiful for each holy season.

In Everyday Life

ACTIVITY Close your eyes. Picture a room in your house. Think about one of the holy seasons. How could you decorate the room for this season? Share your ideas with a partner.

In Your Parish

ACTIVITY
Decorate a church banner for Advent, Christmas, Lent, or Easter. Write the name of the holy season on your banner.

God's Word Teaches Us

Chapter 3

Hear God's Word and keep it.
Then you will be blessed. *Based on* Luke 11:28

Share

We learn in many ways.

Look at the pictures.

Tell how each child learns.

Circle your favorite way to learn.

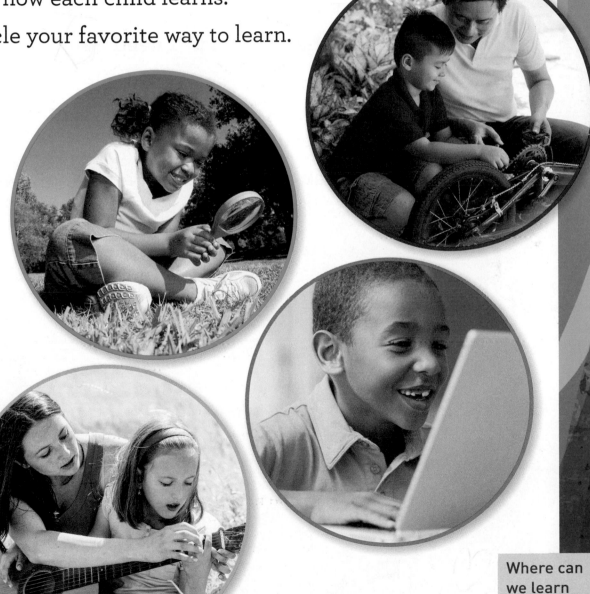

Where can we learn about God?

47

A Man Learns About God

One day a man was on his way home to Africa. He was riding in a chariot. The man was reading his Bible. Philip saw the man and ran up to the chariot.

"Do you understand the Bible?" Philip asked.

"No," the man said. "I need help."

Philip got into the chariot. He told the man about God's love. Philip told the man about Jesus.

The man from Africa became a follower of Jesus. He became a member of the Church.

Based on Acts of the Apostles 8:26–39

Learning About God

The man from Africa wanted to learn about God. Philip helped the man understand the **Bible**. The man became a follower of Jesus.

We listen to the Bible at Mass. The priest or deacon tells us about the Bible story. He helps us learn how to follow Jesus.

Our Church Teaches

The Bible is the written Word of God. God chose special people to write the Bible. Stories in the Bible teach us about God's love. They teach us how to love God and love others. When we listen to the Word of God, we believe God speaks to us. Jesus is also called the Word of God. He teaches us most fully who God is.

When can we hear God's Word?

Saint Augustine

When Augustine was young he often got into trouble. He did many selfish things.

One day Augustine sat in his garden. He was very sad. His good friend had died. Augustine heard a child sing the words, "Take and read!" Augustine saw his mother's Bible on a table. He began to read it. He began to understand God's Word.

Augustine listened carefully to the Bible stories at Mass. He changed his life. He stopped being selfish. Augustine began to follow Jesus.

In what ways did the Word of God change Augustine?

1. At Mass, our parish community listens to God's Word. Draw yourself in the picture. Then draw your family and friends.

2. How can you hear God's Word? Trace the dotted letters to find out.

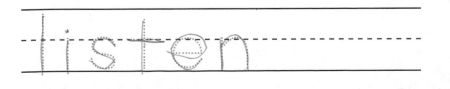

listen

In what ways can God's Word change us?

A Listening Prayer

Leader: O God, open our ears that we may hear.

All: **Help us listen to your Word.**

Leader: Listen to the Word of God. Then think about what you hear.

Reader: Act as God's children. Obey your parents. Love others, just as Jesus did.

Based on Ephesians 5:1; 6:1

Reader: The word of the Lord.

All: **Thanks be to God.**

(Pause)

Leader: O God, happy are we who hear your Word and keep it.

All: **O God, happy are we who hear your Word and keep it. Amen.**

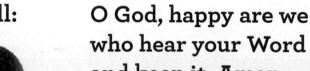

A **Draw** a line to connect the parts of each sentence.

1. God speaks to us through · · Word of God.

2. We hear the Word of God · · the Bible.

3. The Bible is the written · · follow Jesus

4. Augustine read the Bible and began to · · at Mass.

B **Draw or write about** what helped Saint Augustine begin to follow Jesus.

Faith in Action

Priests and Deacons Priests and deacons study the Bible to help us learn to follow Jesus. The deacon at Saint Peter Parish visits the religious education classes. He talks to the children about the Bible readings for Sunday Mass.

In Everyday Life

ACTIVITY

In the Bible Jesus invites us to follow him. Draw a picture that shows one way you have answered Jesus' invitation to follow him.

In Your Parish

ACTIVITY Think about a Bible story read at Mass. What did the priest or deacon say about the story? Share with your class something he said that can help us follow Jesus.

We Give Praise to God

Chapter 4

I will praise the LORD with all my heart . . .

Psalm 111:1

Share

We praise people when they do something good. We say, "Great job!"

Sometimes we praise a person just for being special. We say, "You are wonderful!"

Look at the picture. What do you think is happening?

ACTIVITY

Draw how your face looks when someone praises you.

Why do we praise God?

Hear and Believe Scripture

Praise God!

Everything that God makes
gives him praise.

Give praise to God, sun and moon.

Give praise to God, night and noon.

Give praise to God, mountains tall.

Give praise, people big and small.

Give praise to God, birds that sing.

Give praise to God, everything!

Based on Psalm 148

One Kind of Prayer

God is wonderful! God is good! Everything God made gives him **praise**. Praise is one kind of **prayer**. We praise God to celebrate his goodness.

Some prayers of praise are in the Bible. We can praise God anywhere. We can praise God anytime.

Our Church Teaches

Prayer is listening to and talking to God. We can talk to God with prayers of praise. We can praise God with our parish community. We can tell God that he is good and wonderful.

ACTIVITY

Use the spaces on these pages to draw other things that give praise to God.

We Believe

We listen to and talk to God when we pray. One way to pray is to give praise to God.

Faith Words

praise
Praise is a kind of prayer. It celebrates God's goodness.

prayer
Prayer is listening to and talking to God.

In what ways do we praise God at Mass?

Glory to God

Joey learned about God even before he started school. He learned that God loves us. He learned that all good things come from God.

Now Joey is in the first grade. Each week he goes to Mass with his family. They praise God with their parish community. Sometimes they sing a prayer called the **Gloria**. Joey's favorite words are "Glory to God in the highest, and on earth peace to people of good will."

Roman Missal

Why do you think Joey likes to sing the Gloria?

1. Learn to sign the words "Sing praise to the Lord."

sing   **praise**   **Lord**

2. Read the words that praise God. Then use the numbers on the crayons to help you color the church window.

In what other ways do we praise God?

A Prayer of Praise

Leader: Everything God creates praises him. Let us sign our praise to the Lord.

All (sign): **Sing praise to the Lord.**

Leader: Now let all creation praise God.

Side 1	Side 2
Give praise to God,	**sun and moon.**
Give praise to God,	**night and noon.**
Give praise to God,	**mountains tall.**
Give praise to God,	**people big and small.**
Give praise to God,	**birds that sing.**
Give praise to God,	**everything.**

Based on Psalm 148

All (sing): **Glory to God in the highest, and on earth peace to people of good will.**

A **Circle** the words that best complete the sentences.

1. Prayer is listening to and talking to ——.

   (God)   friends

2. We celebrate God's goodness with prayers of ——.

   sadness   (praise)

3. Some prayers of praise are in the ——.

   sun   (Bible)

4. Everything that God makes gives him ——.

   power   (praise)

5. We can praise God ——.

   (anytime)   only at night

B **Complete** the prayer of praise that we sing at Mass. Write the number of the correct word in each box.

 to 5 in the highest,

and on to 1 of

good will.

1 people

4 peace

5 God

3 Glory

2 earth

Faith in Action

Children's Choir   Some parishes have a children's choir. Boys and girls, small and tall, learn hymns. They practice these songs many times. Then they sing the hymns at Mass. The children praise God when they sing.

In Your Parish

ACTIVITY   Does your parish have a children's choir? Tell about the hymns they sing. What is your favorite hymn? Tell why you like it.

In Everyday Life

ACTIVITY   Learn these words to the unit song, "We Praise You." Sing the words as a prayer. Then color the notes in the border.

We praise you, O Lord,
　　　for all your works are wonderful.
We praise you, O Lord,
　　　forever is your love.

Our Loving God

Jesus taught us that we are all God's special children.
God has given us the gift of his wonderful creation.
We thank God for all the gifts we have received.

"... [L]et us love one another, because
love is of God; ..."   1 John 4:7

Jesus went from town to town around the Sea of Galilee. He taught people about our loving God. When we show our love for others, we follow Jesus.

Come All You People

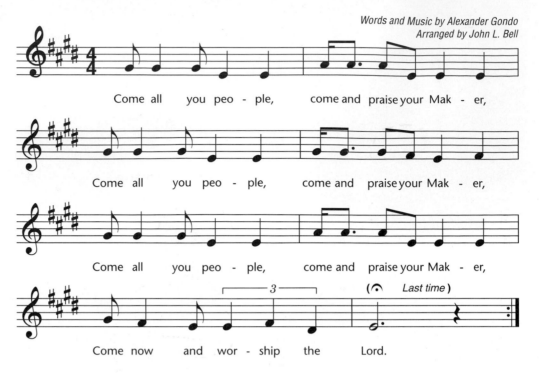

Words and Music by Alexander Gondo
Arranged by John L. Bell

Come all you peo - ple, come and praise your Mak - er,

Come all you peo - ple, come and praise your Mak - er,

Come all you peo - ple, come and praise your Mak - er,

(Last time)

Come now and wor - ship the Lord.

God Is Our Loving Father

Chapter 5

**Praise the LORD, for he is good;
for his mercy endures forever; . . .**

Psalm 136:1

Share

God made all things.

All things show God's love.

Look at the picture.

Tell how each thing
shows God's love.

Draw something you like
that shows God's love.

In what order
did God create
the world?

69

God Creates the World

God made the and at night.

God made the for warmth and light.

And on the land, God planted ,

while in the sky flew and .

The sprang up from the earth.

Sweet and came to birth.

The and swam in the seas.

And on the land were .

Soon and did appear,

with and , and deer.

God Creates People

God saw that everything he created was good. Then God created people to be like himself. God told the people to take care of the fish, the birds, and all the animals.

Based on Genesis 1:26–31

Our Church Teaches

God is our loving Father. He created everything in the world to show his love for us. God cares for us and for all **creation**. God is our **Creator**.

How can we care for God's creation?

Caring for Creation

Anna liked to play in her yard. She liked the little flower garden. Best of all, Anna liked the statue of Saint Francis of Assisi. Anna learned that Francis loved everything God created. Francis took good care of plants. He was kind to animals. He helped people in need.

Anna picked up her watering can. She said, "Thank you, God, for making our world." Then Anna began to water the flowers.

How did Anna care for God's creation?

Here are some ways we can care for God's creation.
Draw a line from each way to its matching picture.

Help people in need.

Be kind to animals.

Take care of
our bodies.

Share God's gifts.

Help our neighbor.

In what ways can
we thank God
for loving us?

Thank You, God!

We can say prayers of thanks. We can say thank you to God for creating the world. We can say thank you to God for creating us.

Leader: For the sun and moon.

All: **Thank you, God.**

Leader: For dry land, mountains, trees, and flowers.

All: **Thank you, God.**

Leader: For oceans and lakes, whales and fish.

All: **Thank you, God.**

Leader: For birds, frogs, horses, and butterflies.

All: **Thank you, God.**

Leader: For our families and for each of us.

All: **Thank you, God.**

Chapter Review

5

Complete the sentences with the words on the flowers.

people love God Francis

1. Our loving Father and Creator is

   God.

2. God created ___People___ to be like himself.

3. God's creation shows his ___Love___ for us.

4. Saint ___Francis___ showed his love for everything that God created.

Faith in *Action*

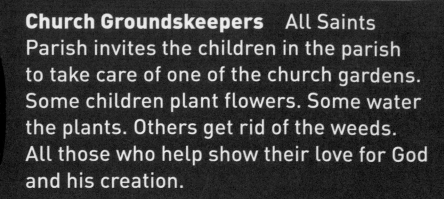

Church Groundskeepers All Saints Parish invites the children in the parish to take care of one of the church gardens. Some children plant flowers. Some water the plants. Others get rid of the weeds. All those who help show their love for God and his creation.

In Everyday Life

ACTIVITY Each day we make choices. Some choices help God's creation. Some choices hurt it. Draw one way you can help God's creation.

In Your Parish

ACTIVITY Picture the grounds around your parish church. What things do you see that were created by God? Tell how the children in your religious education class could care for God's creation.

Baptism Is a Wonderful Gift

Chapter 6

My dear children, the Christian community welcomes you with great joy.

Rite of Baptism

Share

We say "Welcome!" in many ways.

We put up signs. We bring gifts.

We shake hands. We share food.

ACTIVITY

Draw your own welcome picture.

In what ways does the Church welcome us?

79

Baptism Welcomes Us

The Church has a special celebration to welcome new members. We call the celebration Baptism.

The priest or deacon says, "My dear children, the Christian community welcomes you with great joy."

During the celebration the priest or deacon places the person in water or pours water over the person's head three times. He says, "I baptize you in the name of the Father, and of the Son, and of the Holy Spirit."

Rite of Baptism 111, 124

The Celebration of Baptism

The **Sacrament of Baptism** brings us new life in Jesus Christ. We become members of God's family, the Church. Baptism takes away our sins.

Our Church Teaches

In Baptism we become children of God. We become part of God's family. God shares his life with us. He shares his love with us. **Grace** is the gift of God's life in us. Grace fills us with his love. It comes to us through faith in Jesus and the Sacraments. It helps us follow him.

ACTIVITY

Write your first name on the line below. Then color the border.

Rachol

belongs to the Catholic Church!

We Believe

Through Baptism we become children of God and members of the Catholic Church.

Faith Words

Sacrament of Baptism
Baptism is a celebration of welcome into the Catholic community.

grace
Grace is the gift of God's life in us. Grace fills us with his love.

In what ways do Catholics follow Jesus?

Daniel's Baptism

The Riveras adopted Daniel when he was six years old. Last Sunday the whole family took Daniel to church for his Baptism. Father Bob and many people from Saint Dominic's Parish were there. Here are some pictures of Daniel's Baptism. Tell what you see.

After Daniel was baptized the parish community prayed that he would always follow Jesus. Then everyone stood up and clapped to welcome Daniel to the Catholic Church.

How can the people in Saint Dominic's Parish help Daniel be a follower of Jesus?

ACTIVITY

Circle the people who show us ways to follow Jesus.

What reminds us
of our Baptism?

Praying with Holy Water

Leader: Holy Water reminds us of our Baptism. The Sign of the Cross reminds us that we are followers of Jesus.

We will take turns making the Sign of the Cross with Holy Water. We will say this prayer for each person in our class.

All: **Dear God, we ask you to bless (name). Help (name) follow Jesus.**

Leader: Let us together pray the Sign of the Cross.

All: **In the name of the Father, and of the Son, and of the Holy Spirit. Amen.**

Chapter Review

A **Draw a line** to connect the parts of each sentence.

1. In Baptism we become members of the _____ •   • welcome.

2. Baptism is a celebration of _____ •   • grace.

3. The water of Baptism is a sign of new _____ •   • Church.

4. God's loving presence in our lives is called _____ •   • life.

B **Draw or write** about one way a Catholic can follow Jesus.

Faith in Action

Welcoming New Members Each month Saint Paul's Parish welcomes its new members. After Mass the Welcome Group serves coffee and snacks. Everyone gets to meet the new members. They talk about the parish. They talk about their families. They talk about helping others.

In Everyday Life

ACTIVITY Is there a new child in your class or a new family in your neighborhood? On a separate sheet of paper, make a welcome card and give it to them.

In Your Parish

ACTIVITY Make a welcome sign for your church. Draw pictures of people in your parish. Show how your parish is special.

WELCOME

Take Home
Loving God and Others

In this chapter the children will learn that God made us to be loving people. By loving as Jesus did, we will recognize God's image in others and grow in holiness. The children will also learn that God wants us to be happy with him forever in Heaven.

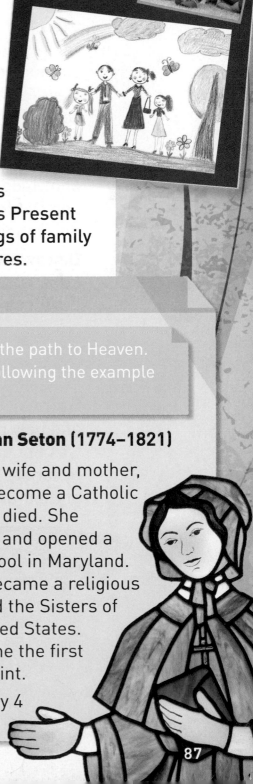

GOD is present in everyone

ACTIVITY **God's Presence**

Explain to your child that God created us and that he is present in each of us. Make a poster and title it "God is Present in Everyone." Help your child attach photos or drawings of family members and friends onto the poster. Label the pictures.

THROUGH THE WEEK

✝ **A PRAYER FOR THE WEEK** Dear God, guide us along the path to Heaven. Help us trust in you and show our love for others by following the example of Saint Elizabeth Ann Seton. Amen.

ON SUNDAY
God is present in everyone in your parish community. At Mass, introduce yourselves to someone you have not met before.

 ON THE WEB
BlestAreWe.com
RCLBLectionary.com
SaintsResource.com

Saint Elizabeth Ann Seton (1774–1821)

Elizabeth Seton, a wife and mother, felt God's call to become a Catholic after her husband died. She became a teacher and opened a Catholic girls' school in Maryland. Elizabeth Seton became a religious sister and founded the Sisters of Charity in the United States. In 1975 she became the first American-born saint.

Feast Day: January 4

Take Home

Scripture Background
In the Time of Jesus

Scribes Scribes were Jewish men capable of reading and writing who were experts in Mosaic law. They studied the Hebrew Scriptures, since they contained so much of the law of Israel. In the New Testament scribes are often seen confronting Jesus on questions of the law. A scribe who questions Jesus in Luke's Gospel demonstrates his knowledge of the Books of Leviticus and Deuteronomy, where the Great Commandment is first found.

Discover the scribe's question by reading Luke 10:25–28, and learn about the law in Leviticus 19:18 and Deuteronomy 6:5.

Our Catholic Tradition **in Holy People**

Saints The Church has canonized, or declared certain good and holy people to be saints. Many saints had ordinary lives. It was not unusual for these good and holy people to be dismissed by family, friends, and even Church officials during much of their lifetimes. The good works of many saints were only acknowledged after their deaths.

All the saints had one thing in common. They lived out the Great Commandment by showing their steadfast love for God and by loving their neighbors as they loved themselves.

Loving God and Others

Beloved, let us love one another, because love is of God; . . .

1 John 4:7

Share

Everything has a purpose.

Circle the things that you would use in a playhouse.

Why did you choose each thing?

ACTIVITY

Draw one more thing to put in a playhouse.

Why did God create us?

89

Scripture

A Man Questions Jesus

Jesus went from town to town teaching the people. One day a man who knew God's law asked Jesus a question.

Man: What must I do to go to Heaven?

Jesus: What is written in the law?

Man: Love God with your whole heart and with your whole mind. Love others as you love yourself.

Jesus: You are right. That is what you must do to go to Heaven.

Based on Luke 10:25–28

Why God Made Us

God created us to be like him. God made us to be good and **holy**. We are good and holy when we love God more than anything else. We are good and holy when we love ourselves. We are good and holy when we love other people. Jesus tells us that this is the way to **Heaven**.

Our Church Teaches

God created us to love him, ourselves, and other people. God made us to be happy with him forever in Heaven.

If we love God and others we will live forever. We will be with Jesus. We will be with all the good and holy people who ever lived. This will be the happiness of Heaven.

ACTIVITY

Find the way to be holy. Color the spaces with an X in purple. Then color the other spaces as you like.

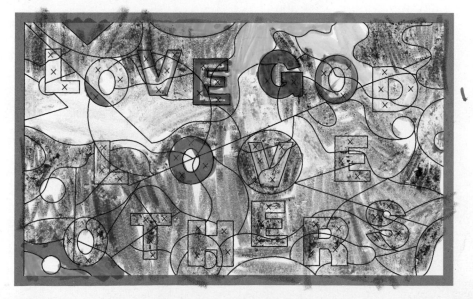

In what other ways can we love ourselves and others?

91

A Holy Man Named Peter

Peter could not think as fast as other people. He spoke very slowly. He walked with a limp. Some people made fun of Peter. But Peter always smiled back.

Peter liked people. He wanted to help them. That is why he liked his job at the grocery store. Peter packed the bags. Then he helped carry them out to the cars.

Peter listened to people's problems. He told the people that God loves them. Peter helped many people feel better.

When Peter died, people were very sad. They said, "Peter was a good and holy man. We were happy to know him."

How was Peter good and holy?

ACTIVITY

Play the game about loving God and other people. Find your way to Jesus.

1. Each player needs a game marker.

2. Toss a penny.

3. Move 1 space for heads or 2 for tails.

Start

You prayed. 1
Go 1 more space.

You shared. 3
Go 1 more space.

2

4

You cared. 5
Go 1 more space.

6

You helped. 7
Go 1 more space.

8

You prayed. 9
Go 1 more space.

Toss heads. 10
Go to Jesus.

Jesus

In what ways can we be good and holy?

93

Praying with Movement

Prayer helps us to be good and holy.

Moving our bodies can help us pray. The words and music of holy songs can help us move.

Let us move our bodies to the words and music of a song of praise.

Write the number of the correct word in each box.
The first one is done for you.

1. God made us to be $\boxed{3}$ and $\boxed{2}$.

2. To be holy is to be like $\boxed{5}$.

3. Jesus tells us to $\boxed{1}$ God, ourselves, and other people.

4. If we do this, we will be $\boxed{6}$ with God forever in $\boxed{4}$.

Faith in *Action*

Parish Greeters One Sunday a month families from Saint Anne's religious education program greet the people going into church. The greeters are friendly. They make the children feel special. Visitors always feel welcome.

In Your Parish

ACTIVITY How do the greeters in your parish make you feel special? How can you help make your parish a friendly place?

In Everyday Life

ACTIVITY God loves you very much. He wants you to love yourself. Then you will be able to love others. Draw a picture of your face in the mirror. Then pray the prayer around your picture.

God, I know that you love me.

Help me to love myself and other people.

We Give Thanks to God

Chapter 8

Thank you, God, for your goodness.
We bless your name.

Based on Psalm 100:4

Share

Aunt Pat helped Nicki and Jenny bake cupcakes. She said they could put on the frosting. Nicki and Jenny surprised Aunt Pat.

ACTIVITY

Color the letters on the cupcakes. How did Nicki and Jenny surprise Aunt Pat?

Why does God give us gifts?

God Is a Good Father

One day Jesus told some people about God.

Jesus: God is like a good father. Imagine that you are a child. You are hungry. You ask your father for a loaf of bread. Will a good father give you a stone?

People: No!

Jesus: What will a good father give you?

People: A loaf of bread.

Jesus: That's right. Now pretend that you ask your father for a fish. Will a good father give you a snake?

People: No!

Jesus: What will a good father give you?

People: A fish.

Jesus: That's right. A good father knows how to give his children what they need. So too, God knows everything you need. God gives good gifts to everyone.

Based on Matthew 7:9–11

God Cares for Us

Jesus told the people that God is like a good father. God knows what everyone needs. He takes care of everyone. God wants us to pray for the things we need. Then God will give us what is good.

Our Church Teaches

Jesus taught us how to pray. He told us to call God our Father. In the **Lord's Prayer** we say, "Our Father who art in heaven, **hallowed** be thy name." We tell God that his name is holy.

Faith Words

Lord's Prayer
The Lord's Prayer is the prayer that Jesus taught us.

hallowed
The word *hallowed* means "holy."

In what ways do we show thanks for God's gifts?

101

The Man Who Said "Thank You"

One day, Jesus met ten people who had a sickness called leprosy. Jesus wanted to show the lepers that God loved them.

Jesus said, "Go to the priests. Your sickness will go away."

All ten lepers did as Jesus said. Along the way, all ten got better. Their leprosy was gone! Nine of them ran off happy. But one man went back to Jesus.

"Thank you," the man said. "I will never forget this wonderful gift."

Then Jesus said, "Go. Your faith has saved you."

Based on Luke 17:11–19

Why was Jesus happy to see the man?

102

1. Trace the letters to complete the prayer.

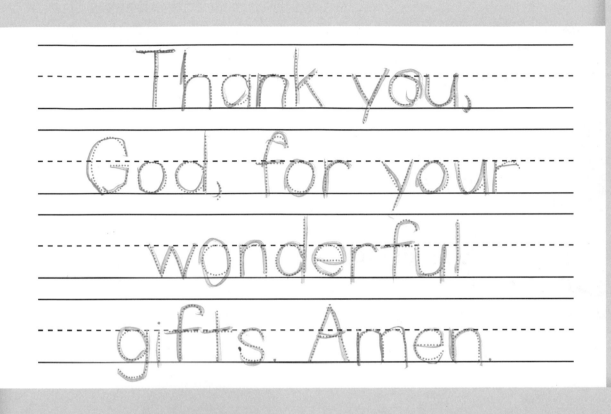

Thank you, God, for your wonderful gifts. Amen.

2. Draw one gift God has given you.

In what ways do we say thank you to God?

A Thank You Prayer

Leader: We can say thank you to God with our hearts. We can say thank you to God with our voices. Let us thank God with our hearts and voices.

Reader 1: God our Father loves us in many ways. Let us thank God with our hearts. *(Pause.)*

Reader 2: God our Father gives us many gifts. Let us thank God with our voices.

Each child: **God our Father, thank you for (name a gift).**

(Conclude by praying the Lord's Prayer.)

Chapter Review 8

A **Draw a line** to connect the parts of each sentence.

1. Jesus taught us to pray the _____   Mass.

2. Hallowed means _____   Lord's Prayer.

3. We pray the Lord's Prayer at _____   holy.

B **Draw or write** about the leper who came back to see Jesus.

Faith in *Action*

Midnight Run   Some parishes collect food and clothes for homeless people in New York City. Homeless people do not have a home to sleep in. Many live on the street or in a park. During the year, members of the Midnight Run group drive into the city to give the food and clothes to the homeless.

In Everyday Life

ACTIVITY   Circle the things that you think homeless people need. Draw a line under two things that you would like to give a homeless person. Ask your family to work together to collect food and clothing for homeless people.

In Your Parish

ACTIVITY   We give thanks to God at Mass for everything we have. Close your eyes and picture the many things that you have. As you picture some of your favorite things, silently pray, "Thank you, God."

God's Son, Jesus

God's greatest gift to us is his Son, Jesus.
Jesus showed us how to be children of God.
Jesus taught us how to care about one another.

Mary and her husband, Joseph, had to travel
to the town of Bethlehem.

Based on Luke 2:1–5

Mary and
Joseph traveled
to Bethlehem
on a road like
this one. Jesus
was born in
Bethlehem.
We joyfully
celebrate the
birth of Jesus.

He Came Down

Traditional from Cameroon
Arranged by John L. Bell

He came down that we may have *love;

He came down that we may have love;

He came down that we may have love,

Cantor
Why did he come?

Hal - le - lu - jah for ev - er - more.

*Substitute peace, joy, hope, life, etc.

Jesus Is God's Son

Praise the God of heaven,
  for his mercy endures forever.

Psalm 136:26

Share

Good news makes people happy.
Look at each picture. Imagine the good
news that each person is hearing.

ACTIVITY

Draw yourself hearing good news.

What good news
did God send?

The Good News

A long time ago God sent the angel Gabriel to Mary. Gabriel had good news for Mary. He told Mary that God wanted her to be the mother of a special baby. God wanted her to name the baby Jesus. This special baby would be the Son of God. Mary said, "Yes. I will do whatever God wants."

Based on Luke 1:26–38

Mary Said Yes

Mary was a young Jewish woman who lived in Nazareth. She was good and holy. Mary listened to the **angel** Gabriel's message. Mary said yes to God. She would be the mother of God's Son. Gabriel told Mary that God would watch over her. Mary trusted God.

Our Church Teaches

God loves us very much. God sent his own Son, **Jesus**, to be our **Savior**. The Son of God became one of us. He shared his life with us. He is always with us.

ACTIVITY Color the letters. Read the words the angel Gabriel said to Mary.

Hail, Mary, full of grace.

We Believe

God asked Mary to be the mother of his Son, Jesus. God sent Jesus to save us.

Faith Words

angel
An angel is a helper or messenger from God.

Savior
Jesus, the Son of God, is our Savior.

In what ways can we share the Good News about Jesus?

Respond # Telling the Good News

David likes his dad to read to him. He loves to hear Bible stories about Jesus. One day David's dad read about the birth of Jesus.

Later that day, David went to play at his friend Mike's house. He told Mike the Good News about Jesus.

What do you think David told his friend?

1. Learn to sign the words "I bring you Good News."
   Then share Good News about Jesus with others.

| I | bring | you | Good | News. |

2. How would you share the Good News of Jesus with others? Draw a picture that shows you sharing the Good News.

In what ways can we celebrate the Good News about Jesus?

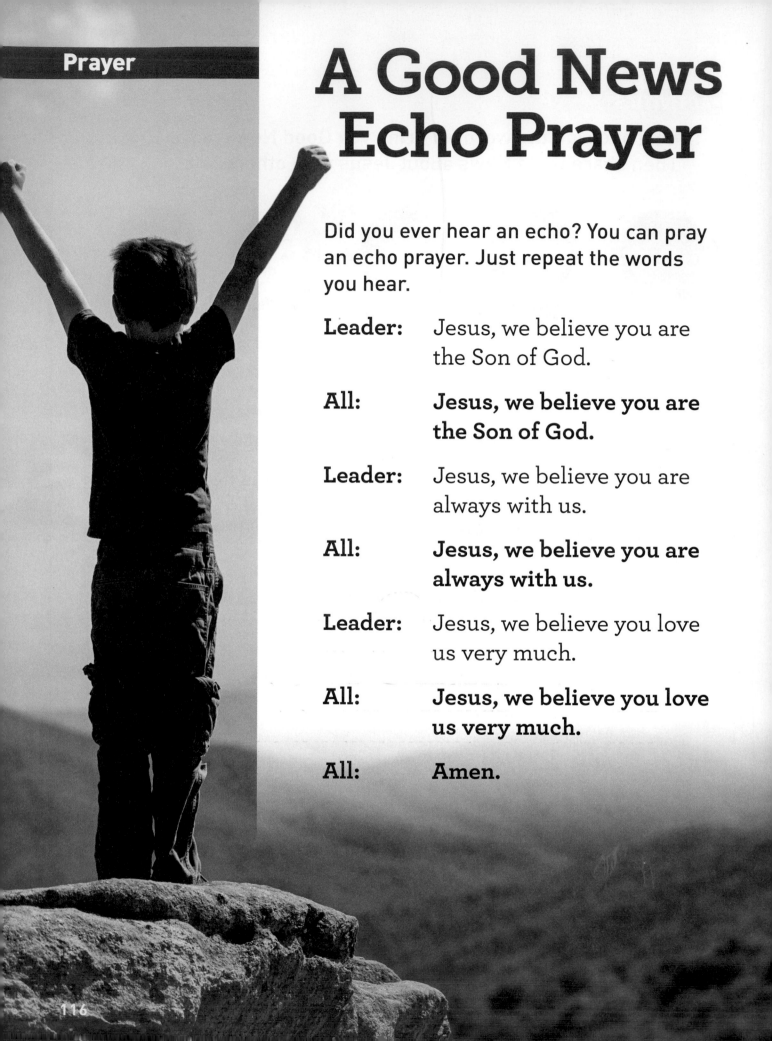

A Good News Echo Prayer

Did you ever hear an echo? You can pray an echo prayer. Just repeat the words you hear.

Leader: Jesus, we believe you are the Son of God.

All: **Jesus, we believe you are the Son of God.**

Leader: Jesus, we believe you are always with us.

All: **Jesus, we believe you are always with us.**

Leader: Jesus, we believe you love us very much.

All: **Jesus, we believe you love us very much.**

All: **Amen.**

A **Draw** a line to connect the parts of each sentence.

1. An angel is a • • own Son.

2. Jesus' mother is • • our Savior.

3. Jesus is God's • • Mary.

4. God sent Jesus to be • • helper or messenger from God.

B **Write** something that you can tell others about the Good News of Jesus' birth.

_____

- -

_____

_____

- -

_____

_____

- -

_____

_____

- -

_____

Faith in *Action*

Shawl Ministry Women in Holy Family Parish knit shawls for people who are sick or lonely. The knitters pray for the people who will get the shawls. Children in the parish religious education program make cards to go with the shawls.

In Everyday Life

ACTIVITY Jesus showed us how to love and respect our families and friends. This week share the Good News of Jesus Christ. Do something special for a family member without telling him or her about it. Doing an extra chore, sharing your things with your brother or sister, and giving time to a grandparent are some examples of things you might do.

In Your Parish

ACTIVITY How does your parish show that it cares for people who are sick and lonely? Write a note to a sick or lonely person. Tell the person that you will pray for him or her.

We Celebrate the Gift of Eucharist

Chapter 10

... "This is my body, which will be given for you; do this in memory of me."

Luke 22:19

Share

Special meals can be fun.

There is good food.

There are people we like.

ACTIVITY

Circle the foods you like.

Plan a special meal for your family.
Draw the food you would like at this special meal.

What special meal did Jesus eat with his friends?

Hear and Believe   Worship

A Special Meal

On the night before he died Jesus ate a special meal with his friends. We call this meal the Last Supper. Here is what Jesus said and did.

Jesus took bread from the table. He gave God thanks and praise. Then he broke the bread. He gave it to his friends and said, "Take this, all of you, and eat of it, for this is my Body."

When supper was ended, Jesus took a cup of wine. He thanked God. He gave the cup to his friends and said, "Take this, all of you, and drink from it, for this is the chalice of my blood."

Based on the Eucharistic Prayer, *Roman Missal*

Jesus with Us

At the **Last Supper**, Jesus shared the gift of himself with his friends. Today, Jesus comes to us in the **Eucharist**. In the Eucharist we share a holy meal. We celebrate that Jesus' sacrifice on the Cross is made present again. We thank God for giving us the Body and Blood of Christ in the Eucharist.

Our Church Teaches

Jesus Christ is present in the Eucharist. **Christ** is another name for Jesus. It reminds us that Jesus was sent by God to save all people.

When Catholics receive Holy Communion they receive the Body and Blood of Jesus Christ. After Mass the Eucharist is kept in the **tabernacle**.

In what way can we show our love for Christ in the Eucharist?

Respond Saint Katharine Drexel

As a child, Katharine went to Mass with her family. She knew that the bread and wine are changed into the Body and Blood of Christ. Katharine learned that the Eucharist in the tabernacle is called the **Blessed Sacrament**.

Katharine's parents helped people in need. Katharine wanted to help, too.

When she grew up, Katharine helped Native Americans and African Americans. She paid to have schools built for them.

Katharine started a community called the Sisters of the Blessed Sacrament. She and the sisters taught others about the Eucharist. They shared the Good News about Jesus.

How did Katharine show her love for Jesus?

1. **These objects help us remember Jesus. Connect the dots. What do you see?**

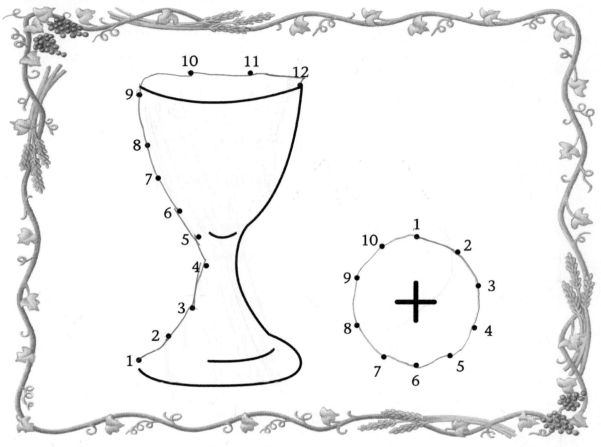

2. **Do you remember what Jesus said at the Last Supper? Finish the sentences.**

Take this, all of you, and eat of it, for this is my

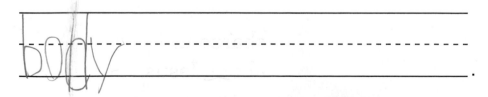

body

Take this, all of you, and drink from it, for this is the chalice of my

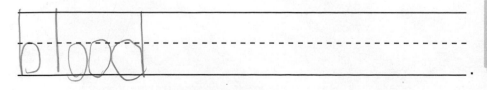

blood

> What are some ways we pray before the Blessed Sacrament?

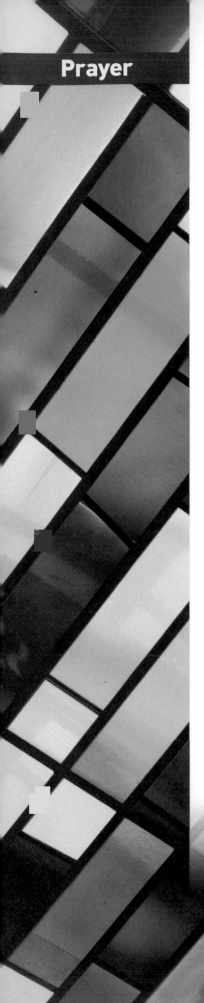

A Prayer of Adoration

We **adore** Jesus Christ by kneeling or bowing before the Blessed Sacrament.

Leader: Come let us adore the Lord, and bow down in worship. *(All bow.)*

All: **Lord, we adore you.** *(All rise.)*

Leader: Let us kneel before the Lord on the left knee. *(All kneel.)*

All: **Lord, we adore you.** *(All stand.)*

Leader: Let us kneel before the Lord on the right knee. *(All kneel.)*

All: **Lord, we adore you.** *(All stand.)*

Leader: Let us kneel before the Lord on both knees. *(All kneel.)*

All: **Lord, we adore you.** *(All stand.)*

Based on Psalm 95:6–7 and the Maronite Rite of Kneeling

A **Complete** the sentences with words from the box.

Sacrament	Jesus	Last Supper

1. The _Last Supper_
is a special meal Jesus shared with his friends.

2. We believe _Jesus_
is present in the Eucharist.

3. Katharine Drexel started the Sisters of the Blessed
Sacrament

B **Draw or write about** how you can adore Jesus in the Blessed Sacrament.

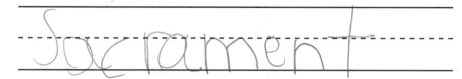

blood

Faith in *Action*

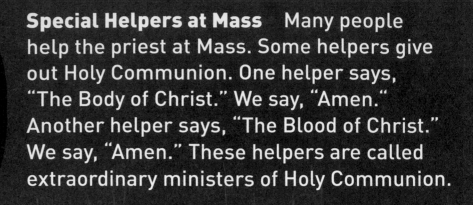

Special Helpers at Mass Many people help the priest at Mass. Some helpers give out Holy Communion. One helper says, "The Body of Christ." We say, "Amen." Another helper says, "The Blood of Christ." We say, "Amen." These helpers are called extraordinary ministers of Holy Communion.

In Your Parish

ACTIVITY Some special helpers take the Eucharist to sick people. Use the code to complete the sentence below. The Eucharist for sick people is kept in the

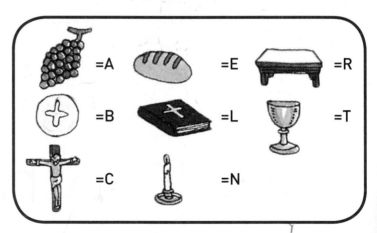

=A
=E
=R
=B
=L
=T
=C
=N

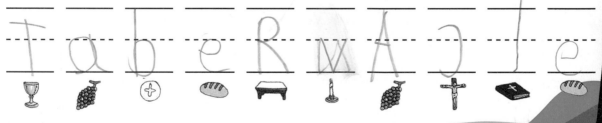

Tabernacle

In Everyday Life

ACTIVITY The things we eat at mealtimes feed our bodies. At Mass, the Eucharist feeds our spirits. Think of a way you and your family can help feed those who do not have enough to eat.

Forgive me, O God, for I have done wrong.

Based on Luke 18:13

Share

Sometimes we do what is right.

Sometimes we do what is wrong.

Look at these pictures.

Draw a if the action is right.

Draw a if the action is wrong.

What does Jesus teach us to do?

131

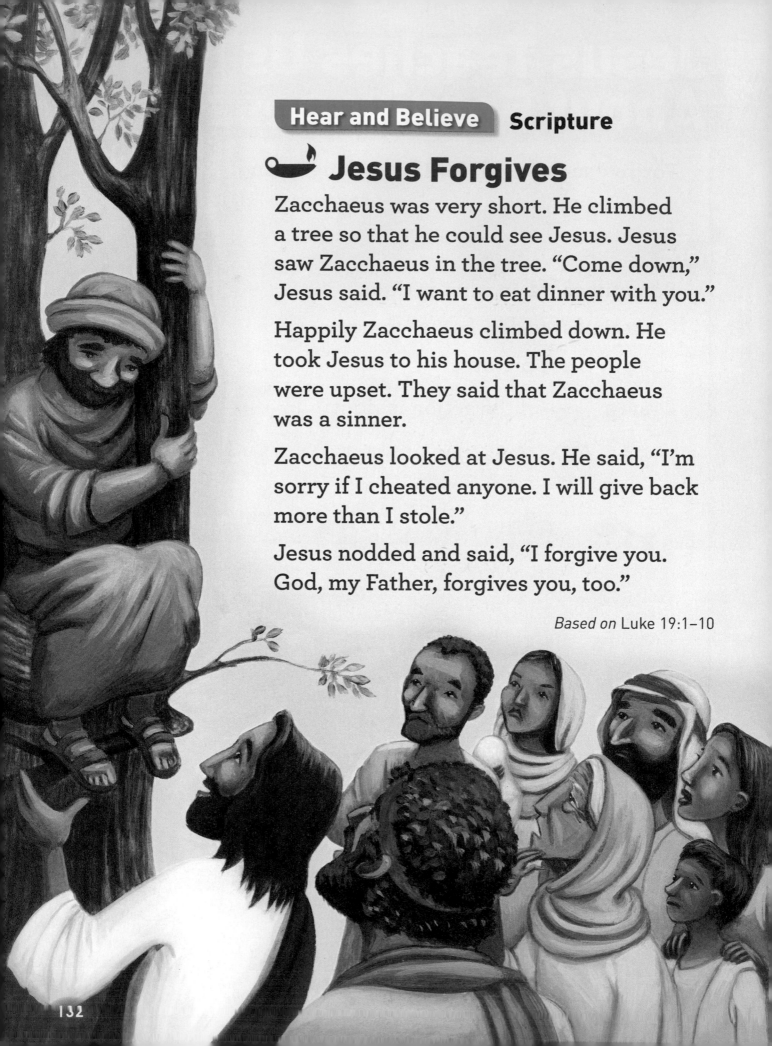

Jesus Forgives

Zacchaeus was very short. He climbed a tree so that he could see Jesus. Jesus saw Zacchaeus in the tree. "Come down," Jesus said. "I want to eat dinner with you."

Happily Zacchaeus climbed down. He took Jesus to his house. The people were upset. They said that Zacchaeus was a sinner.

Zacchaeus looked at Jesus. He said, "I'm sorry if I cheated anyone. I will give back more than I stole."

Jesus nodded and said, "I forgive you. God, my Father, forgives you, too."

Based on Luke 19:1–10

What Jesus Wants

Zacchaeus was a selfish man. But he was sorry and began to help others. Jesus loved Zacchaeus and forgave him. Jesus teaches us to love God and others. When we do not act in a loving way, God wants us to be sorry. God will always **forgive** us.

Our Church Teaches

Jesus wants us to obey God's laws. The laws of God help us choose to do what is right. When we choose to do what is wrong, we **sin**. When we sin we turn away from God. Sin also hurts our friendship with other people. But God never stops loving us. He is always ready to forgive us.

ACTIVITY Draw a picture of Jesus and Zaccheus eating dinner.

In what ways can we forgive someone?

133

A Forgiveness Story

Jake played his video game over and over again. His mom told him to stop. She told Jake to do his homework. Jake was angry and said something mean to his mom. So she sent him to his room.

Jake lay on his bed. He heard his parents talking. He heard his little sisters playing. He wanted to be with them. But soon Jake fell asleep.

When Jake awoke, he saw a sandwich on his table. Next to the sandwich was a note from his mom.

What do you think the note said?

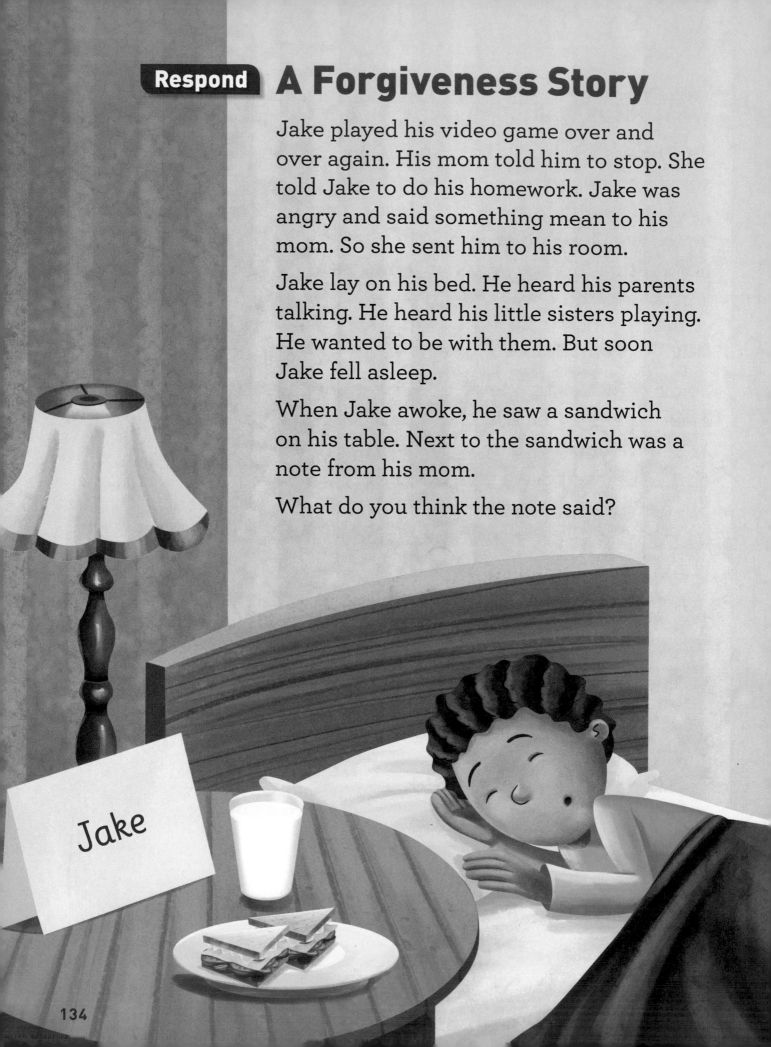

Jake

1. **Write the answers on the lines.**

   If you hurt someone, what can you say?

   <u>I'm sorry</u>

   Someone is sorry for hurting you.
   What can you say?

   <u>I forgive you</u>

2. **Jake read his mom's note. Draw a picture of what you think Jake did next.**

How can we celebrate God's forgiveness?

A Prayer for God's Mercy

At Mass we tell God we are sorry for our sins. Then we pray for God's **mercy**, or loving forgiveness.

Leader: Let us bow our heads and think about ways we have failed to love God and others. *(Pause.)*

Leader: For the times we have hurt others,

All: **Lord, have mercy.**

Leader: For the times we have not told the truth,

All: **Christ, have mercy.**

Leader: For the times we have not said "I am sorry,"

All: **Lord, have mercy.**

Chapter Review

A **Draw a line** to connect the parts of each sentence.

1. Jesus wants us to obey _____   loving us.

2. A choice to do something that we know is wrong is _____   God's laws.

3. Zaccheus told Jesus that he was _____   a sin.

4. God never stops _____   sorry.

B **Draw a line** to match each picture to the words.

"I'm sorry, Mom."

"I forgive you."

"Lord, have mercy."

Faith in Action

Parish Staff Each parish has workers who do important jobs. The office manager answers the phone, types the parish bulletin, and keeps the list of parish members up to date. The custodian cleans the church and makes sure the lights, heat, and air conditioner work. All parish workers should be respected and treated fairly.

In Everyday Life

ACTIVITY

People work to get the money for things they need for themselves and for their families. People need food, water, a house, clothes, books, and a doctor's care. Find and circle pictures of things that take care of these needs.

In Your Parish

ACTIVITY Who are some of the workers in your parish? What jobs do they do? How can your parish show respect for its workers?

We Pray with God's Word

Chapter 12

..."Lord, teach us to pray..."

Luke 11:1

Share

People pray in many ways.
Think about how you pray.
How do you talk to and listen to God?

Mark an X in each picture that shows how you pray.

Circle your favorite way to pray.

In what ways did Jesus pray?

⚱ Jesus Prayed

The Bible tells us how and where Jesus prayed. He prayed with his heart and his voice. He prayed with his mind.

Jesus prayed with his family in the **Temple**. Jesus prayed alone in the desert. Sometimes he prayed on a mountain. Sometimes he prayed in a boat.

After the Last Supper, Jesus sang the **psalms** with his friends. Then he went into a garden to pray.

The Temple in Jerusalem
Luke 2:41–52

The Desert
Luke 4:1

The Mountains
Matthew 14:23

Praying Like Jesus

We can learn to pray like Jesus. We can pray aloud with our voices. We can pray silently with our hearts and minds. We can pray alone or with other people. We can pray anywhere and anytime.

Our Church Teaches

We can pray with **Gospel** stories from the Bible. There are four Gospels. They are the Good News of Jesus. They tell us how to show our love for God and other people. We grow closer to Jesus when we pray with the Gospels.

The Sea of Galilee
Matthew 14:13

The Garden of Gethsemane
Matthew 26:30

What are some ways we can we pray with a Gospel story?

Praying with God's Word

There are four steps in praying with a Gospel story. Let's go through them together.

Step 1: **Relax**

Close your eyes.
Become quiet.
Ask God to fill your
heart and mind.

Step 2: **Look and Listen**

Look at the picture of
Jesus and the children.
Listen to the Bible story.

 Jesus Blesses the Children

Jesus had been teaching all day. He was tired and sat down to rest.

Many parents started to bring their children to Jesus. They wanted Jesus to bless the children. But Jesus' friends told the people not to bother Jesus.

When Jesus saw this, he said, "Don't stop them. Let the children come closer. I love little children." Then Jesus placed his hands on the children. He gave them his blessing.

Based on Mark 10:13–16

Step 3: Imagine

Imagine that you are going to see Jesus.
He is on a hillside with his friends.
Jesus is sitting under a tree.

Step 4: Think

Put yourself in the story. Ask yourself these questions.

Does Jesus see you?
Do you go up to him?
What do you say to Jesus?
What does Jesus say to you?

Draw yourself in the
picture with Jesus
and the children.

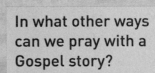

In what other ways
can we pray with a
Gospel story?

A Thank You Prayer

You have learned to pray with God's Word in the Bible. Acting out stories in the Bible can help you pray, too.

Act out the story of Jesus blessing the children. Then say this prayer together.

Thank you, Jesus, for loving us. Amen.

A **Circle** the word that best completes each sentence.

1. Jesus prayed with his family in the _____ .

   park   (Temple)

2. Prayers that we can sing are called _____ .

   (psalms)   the Bible

3. The Gospel is the Good News of _____ .

   Moses   (Jesus)

4. We can _____ with a Gospel story.

   (pray)   play

B **Write or draw** about how you like to pray.

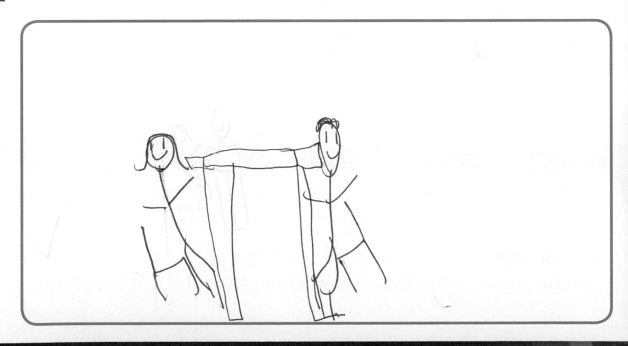

Faith in *Action*

Praying with Scripture Each week in many parishes, small groups gather to pray. They read the Scripture readings for the next Sunday's Mass. They think about the readings. They share their thoughts. Then they pray about how they can show their love for God and others.

In Everyday Life

ACTIVITY We are all part of God's family. When a family member is in need, we can reach out by praying for his or her needs. Write a prayer for someone in need. Pray it tonight with your family.

_____

- -

_____
_____

- -

_____

- -

_____

In Your Parish

ACTIVITY Think of questions to ask a prayer group in the parish. Plan to tell how you pray with a Gospel story.

The Holy Spirit

Jesus sends us the Holy Spirit to help us live as Jesus' followers. Sometimes it is hard to know what God wants us to do. We can pray to the Holy Spirit for help.

If we live in the Spirit, let us also follow the Spirit.

Galatians 5:25

Paul sailed to different cities in a boat like this one. He taught people that the Holy Spirit is our helper. When we love others the Holy Spirit helps us to be kind.

If You Believe and I Believe

Traditional from Zimbabwe
Arranged by John L. Bell

If you be-lieve— and I be-lieve And we to-geth-er pray,——

The Ho - ly Spir - it must come down And set God's peo - ple free,——

And set God's peo - ple free,—— And set God's peo - ple free;——

The Ho - ly Spir - it must come down And

set God's peo - ple free.——

Take Home

Jesus Promises the Holy Spirit

In this chapter the children will read about Jesus' promise to send the Holy Spirit. They will learn that the Holy Spirit is the gift of God's love. They will discover that the Holy Spirit helps us remember Jesus' teachings. Together they will praise God the Father, Son, and Holy Spirit.

ACTIVITY **A Welcome Sign**

Showing a spirit of hospitality is one way to share love with others. Invite a family from your parish or neighborhood to your home for dinner or dessert. In preparation, discuss with your child the importance of hospitality. Together, make a welcome sign for the family you invite.

THROUGH THE WEEK

✝ **A PRAYER FOR THE WEEK** Come, Holy Spirit, fill our hearts with your gifts of love and peace. Help us follow the example of Saint Dominic Savio by being a sign of peace to everyone we meet. Amen.

ON SUNDAY
One image of the Holy Spirit is the dove. Look for other images of the Holy Spirit in your church.

🖥 **ON THE WEB**
BlestAreWe.com
RCLBLectionary.com
SaintsResource.com

Saint Dominic Savio (1842–1857)

Dominic Savio was born in Italy. At the time of his First Holy Communion he considered Jesus and Mary to be his best friends. Dominic liked to pray and study, and was viewed as a peacemaker at his school. He became ill and died before his fifteenth birthday.

Patron Saint of: young boys
Feast Day: March 9

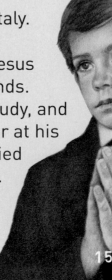

Take Home

Scripture Background
In the Time of Jesus

The Advocate In the Last Supper discourses in the Gospel of John (see John 14:15–31), Jesus makes a promise to his disciples. Jesus says that after his departure he will send another Advocate—himself being the first—to remain with them. Jesus specifies the conditions for receiving the Advocate: their love for him and the keeping of his Commandments. This Advocate is clearly the Holy Spirit, the "Spirit of Truth," who after Jesus' Death and Resurrection will continue his work by helping the disciples understand the meaning of Jesus' teachings and example.

Our Catholic Tradition **in Symbols**

The Dove The image of the dove, which is a symbol of Baptism, appears in the Old Testament in the story of Noah. At Jesus' Baptism by John, the Holy Spirit descended upon him like a dove (see Matthew 3:16). Similarly, the Holy Spirit comes to us in Baptism and remains in us to guide our actions. As a sign of the union of the Holy Spirit and Jesus Christ, receptacles for the Eucharist that would be taken to the dying were made in the shape of a dove. The containers were hung above the altar in many churches, beginning in the early Middle Ages. They were originally made of precious metal—usually gold or silver. Later the dove was made of different materials, including gilded leather. The dove became the outer vessel holding the smaller container, or *pyx*, with the Blessed Sacrament inside.

Jesus Promises the Holy Spirit

My Father will send you a helper to be with you always.

Based on John 14:16

Share

Your family loves you very much.
Your family helps you in many ways.
Your family needs helpers to care
for you and to help you learn.

ACTIVITIES

Tell how each person helps you.

STOP

Write about a person who helps you.

_____

- -

_____

_____

- -

_____

Who is the helper
Jesus asked his
Father to send?

153

A Special Helper

The friends of Jesus were sad. They did not want Jesus to leave them. "Stay with us," they begged.

Jesus shook his head. "I must go away, but I will not leave you alone. I will ask God the Father to send you the Holy Spirit."

"Who is the Holy Spirit?" they asked.

"The Holy Spirit is the helper God the Father will send to those who love me," Jesus said. "The Holy Spirit will teach you more about God's love. The Holy Spirit will help you remember all that I have told you."

Jesus' friends looked worried.

"Don't be afraid," Jesus said. "The Holy Spirit will bring you peace. He will always be with you."

Based on John 14:15–31

Jesus' Promise

Jesus promised his friends that he would not leave them alone. He promised to send the **Holy Spirit** to be their helper. The Holy Spirit is our helper too. The Holy Spirit helps us grow in God's love. He helps us love others. The Holy Spirit brings us peace.

Our Church Teaches

God the Holy Spirit is the gift of God's love to us. The Holy Spirit is always with us. He helps us and guides us.

We Believe

The Holy Spirit is always with us. The Holy Spirit helps us and guides us.

Faith Words

Holy Spirit
The Holy Spirit is God. The Holy Spirit helps us follow Jesus.

ACTIVITY

Color the word that tells what the Holy Spirit brings to us.

PEACE

In what other ways can the Holy Spirit help us?

Abbey's Problem

One morning Abbey was waiting for the school bus. Something very scary happened. Two older boys pushed a first grade boy into the street. The older boys thought it was funny. They began to laugh.

When Abbey got to school, she told her teacher what happened. Abbey was afraid that the other children might tease her.

That night Abbey's mother said, "You did the right thing. Your teacher will know how to handle the problem."

At bedtime Abbey's mother taught her this prayer. "Holy Spirit, help me always do what is right."

Why did Abbey's mother teach her this prayer?

1. Color the border around the prayer.
   Then pray the prayer.

**Holy Spirit,
help me always do
what is right.**

2. Look at each picture. Circle the choice the
   Holy Spirit will help the children make.

to cheat

to be honest

to make peace

to fight

In what ways can we
celebrate God's gift of
the Holy Spirit?

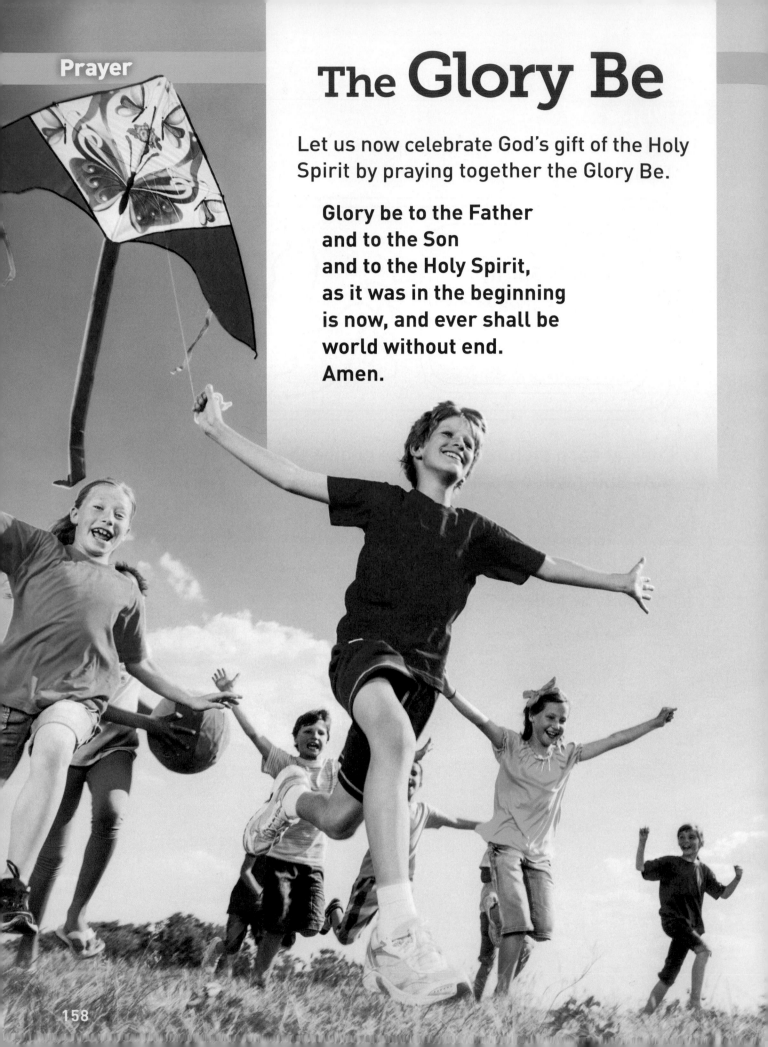

The Glory Be

Let us now celebrate God's gift of the Holy Spirit by praying together the Glory Be.

**Glory be to the Father
and to the Son
and to the Holy Spirit,
as it was in the beginning
is now, and ever shall be
world without end.
Amen.**

Chapter Review 13

A **Draw a line** to connect the parts of each sentence.

1. Jesus promised to send • • God's love.

2. The Holy Spirit helps us • • the Holy Spirit.

3. The Holy Spirit is a gift of • • with us.

4. The Holy Spirit is always • • follow Jesus.

B **Circle** the words that name choices the Holy Spirit helps people make.

1. Gabby will _____ at home.

   help   be lazy

2. José will _____ when he plays with his friends.

   cheat   be fair

3. Kim will _____ at Mass.

   play   pray

4. David will _____ at school.

   listen   not listen

Faith in Action

Parents   Some men and women are called to be parents. The Holy Spirit gives parents special gifts. These gifts help parents share their love and their faith with their children.

In Everyday Life

ACTIVITY   The Holy Spirit helps us share our faith with others. What will you tell someone in your family about Jesus this week?

In Your Parish

ACTIVITY   What kinds of activities are there for families in your parish? Draw a picture of your favorite one.

God's Gift of the Holy Spirit

Chapter 14

O God, send your Holy Spirit to help and guide us.
Based on the *Order of Confirmation*

Share

Water and oil are used in many ways. Circle the sign for water or oil under each picture.

water

oil

In what ways does the Church use water and oil?

The Gift of the Holy Spirit

We receive the gift of the Holy Spirit in the **Sacraments**. Two of the Sacraments are Baptism and Confirmation.

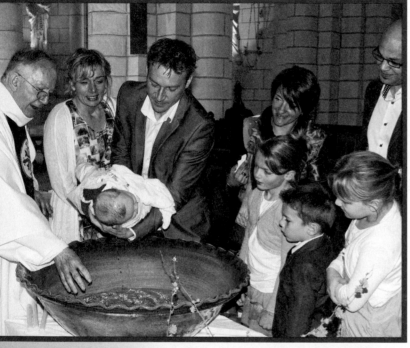

The priest or deacon blesses the water before he baptizes someone with it. He prays, "Father, by the power of the Holy Spirit, we ask you now to bless this water. May it wash away all sin and give us new life in Christ."

Based on the
Rite of Baptism for Children

In Confirmation, the Bishop makes the sign of the cross on the forehead of the person being confirmed. He says, "Be sealed with the Gift of the Holy Spirit." This means "Be filled with God's Spirit."

Based on the *Order of Confirmation*

The Holy Spirit Comes to Us

The Holy Spirit comes to us in the Sacraments. The Church celebrates the Sacraments as signs of God's love. In each Sacrament the Holy Spirit gives us grace. This gift of grace helps us follow Jesus.

Our Church Teaches

In the Sacrament of Baptism we are washed clean of all sin. The water is a sign of new life. The Holy Spirit fills us with God's love. The Holy Spirit helps us live as good Catholics.

In the Sacrament of **Confirmation**, the Holy Spirit makes our faith in Jesus Christ stronger. Confirmation completes the grace of our Baptism. The bishop or priest says words and anoints us with holy oil.

We Believe

We receive the Holy Spirit in the Sacraments. The Holy Spirit helps us live as followers of Jesus.

Faith Words

Sacraments
The Sacraments are special signs of God's love.

Confirmation
Confirmation is the Sacrament in which the Holy Spirit makes our faith in Jesus Christ stronger.

In what other ways can the Holy Spirit help us?

The Story of Nicodemus

One night Nicodemus went secretly to Jesus. "What must I do to become a member of God's kingdom?" he asked Jesus.

Jesus said, "You must be born of water and the Spirit."

"How can this happen?" Nicodemus asked.

Jesus explained, "If you believe in me, the Holy Spirit will bring you God's own life. This life will last forever."

"What is this life like?" Nicodemus asked.

Jesus explained, "Instead of living in darkness, you will live in the light. Instead of doing bad things, you will do what is good."

Based on John 3:1–21

What do you think Nicodemus did next?

ACTIVITY

The Holy Spirit guides us to make good choices. Look at each picture. Read the sentences. Draw a line under the better choice.

Please take out the garbage.

Lily watches TV.
Lily takes out the garbage.

It's my turn to play.

Tim keeps playing with the truck.
Tim lets Bruce play with the truck.

Pray with us.

Rosa tries to sing and pray.
Rosa talks in church.

In what ways do we pray to the Holy Spirit?

167

A Prayer to the Holy Spirit

Special prayers are said when holy oil is used in the Sacraments. We can pray with oil too. The oil reminds us that the Holy Spirit is with us.

Leader: Let us call upon the Holy Spirit to help us follow Jesus.

All: **Holy Spirit, help us and guide us.**

Leader: *(Rub oil on each child's hands.)*

The Holy Spirit lives in you. What is your prayer?

Child: **Holy Spirit, help me and guide me.**

Chapter Review

A **Circle the word** that best completes each sentence.

1. We are washed clean of all sin in _____ .

   Confirmation   Baptism

2. Special signs of God's love are called the _____ .

   prayers   Sacraments

3. The Sacrament that makes our faith in Jesus Christ stronger is _____ .

   Confirmation   Penance

4. Jesus told Nicodemus that God's life lasts _____ .

   forever   ten years

B **Draw or write** about a time when the Holy Spirit helped you.

Faith in Action

Altar Servers Boys and girls can usually become altar servers in the fourth grade. An altar server carries the crucifix in the entrance procession and helps set the altar for the Liturgy of the Eucharist. He or she may also hold candles at the ambo as the Gospel is proclaimed by the priest or deacon.

In Your Parish

ACTIVITY

In each corner of the maze there is something to bring to the altar. Draw a line along the right path from each object to the altar.

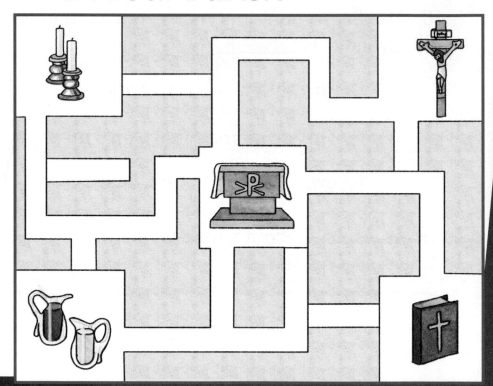

In Everyday Life

ACTIVITY Name two ways that you can serve, or help, your family at home this week. Name two ways you can serve at school this week.

The Holy Spirit Is Our Helper

Chapter 15

> . . . [L]et us also follow the Spirit.
>
> Galatians 5:25

Share

Some things we do are habits. Our habits can be good or bad. To brush our teeth every day is a good habit. To bite our nails is a bad habit.

ACTIVITY

Write a **G** in the box before Nick and Isabel's good habits.

Write a **B** in the box before Nick and Isabel's bad habits.

 Isabel puts her toys away before bedtime.

 Nick always leaves his jacket on the floor.

 Nick says thank you when he gets a gift.

 Isabel prays to God each day.

 Isabel slams the door every morning.

What good habits does the Holy Spirit help us learn?

173

A Letter from Paul

Paul became a follower of Jesus Christ. He wrote this letter to a group of the first **Christians.**

My Dear People,

Jesus Christ loves you. He wants you to love others the way you love yourselves. Sometimes it will be hard to be kind and helpful. But Christ gave you the Holy Spirit to be your helper and guide.

If you follow the Spirit, the **Fruits of the Holy Spirit** will be yours. You will act with love, joy, and peace. You will be patient, gentle, and kind. You will have self-control.

Based on Galatians 5:14–25

Joy

Peace

Love

Self-Control

Kindness

Patience

Gentleness

The Holy Spirit Helps Us

Paul's letter is about loving others. Jesus knew that it would not always be easy to love. That is why Jesus gave us the Holy Spirit. When we love others, the Holy Spirit helps us to be joyful, peaceful, patient, gentle, and kind. He helps us to use self-control.

Our Church Teaches

When we practice good habits, we share the Fruits of the Holy Spirit with others. These Fruits are signs that the Holy Spirit is acting in our lives. When we do kind acts again and again, kindness becomes a habit. Our kindness teaches others about the kindness of God.

ACTIVITY Which Fruit of the Holy Spirit would help each child? Circle the names of these Fruits on Paul's scroll.

We Believe

The Holy Spirit helps us follow Jesus. The Holy Spirit helps us learn good habits of showing love for others.

Faith Words

Christians
Christians are people who love Jesus Christ and follow him.

Fruits of the Holy Spirit
The Fruits of the Holy Spirit are signs that he is acting in our lives.

In what ways can we use the Fruits of the Holy Spirit?

Anthony's Saturday Habit

Anthony is fun to play with. He shares his toys. He helps younger children learn new games. He stops fights by saying funny things. Everyone feels good when Anthony is around. But Anthony has a Saturday habit. He plays video games for three hours. All his neighborhood friends want him to come out and play. But Anthony says, "I can't. I need to finish my game."

What do you think about Anthony's habit?

patience

joy

peace

kindness

self-control

love

gentleness

ACTIVITIES

1. Pick a Fruit of the Holy Spirit and circle it. Draw how you will use this Fruit with someone at home.

2. Pick another Fruit of the Holy Spirit and draw a box around it. Write about how you will use this Fruit in school.

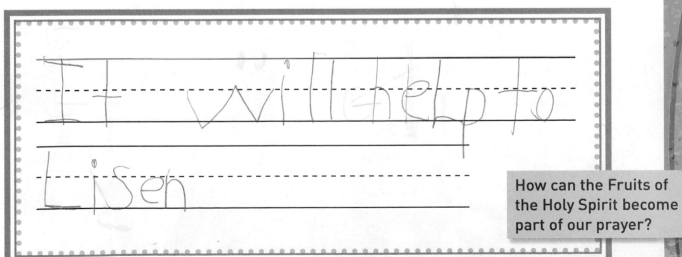

It will help to Lisen

How can the Fruits of the Holy Spirit become part of our prayer?

A Prayer to the Holy Spirit

Leader: Let us pray to the Holy Spirit, our helper and guide. Let us ask the Holy Spirit to help us use the Fruits of kindness, joy, peace, gentleness, and love.

Side 1: When a new child moves into our neighborhood,

Side 2: **help us show kindness.**

Side 1: When our friends are sad,

Side 2: **help us bring them joy.**

Side 1: When children are fighting,

Side 2: **help us bring about peace.**

Side 1: When someone is hurting,

Side 2: **help us show gentleness.**

Leader: Holy Spirit, fill us with your love. Help us show love for others.

All: **Amen.**

Chapter Review 15

Complete the sentences with words from the box.

Fruits   kind   Christians   Jesus Christ   joy

1. People who love and follow Jesus Christ

   are called _Christians_.

2. Paul's letter tells us that

   Joy loves us.

3. The _Fruits_ of the
   Holy Spirit are signs that he is acting in our lives.

4. The Holy Spirit helps us to be

   Fruits to others.

5. The Holy Spirit helps us share our love and

   _____ with others.

Faith in *Action*

Youth Group   Many parishes have a group for teens. The teens pray together and learn more about God. They take part in parish activities and serve their communities. In a parish youth group, the teens make new friends.

In Your Parish

ACTIVITY   Does your parish have a youth group? How do the teens help others? Share what you know with a partner.

In Everyday Life

ACTIVITY   The Holy Spirit helps us act in good ways. Read the signs. Circle one way that you would like to act. Then draw yourself acting in this way.

Help a friend

Obey your parents

Pray every day

Share

Forgive others

Take Home

The Holy Spirit Helps Us Pray

In this chapter the children will read some of Jesus' teachings about prayer. They will learn that the Holy Spirit teaches us how to pray. The children will write prayers of petition to the Holy Spirit.

ACTIVITY **A Prayer Box**

Decorate a small box with symbols of the Holy Spirit. Leave blank slips of paper next to the box. Invite family members to write petitions on the papers and to place them in the prayer box. Together, read the petitions and pray, "Holy Spirit, help us."

THROUGH THE WEEK

✝ **A PRAYER FOR THE WEEK** Come Holy Spirit, fill our family with your love. Help us place our trust in Jesus and show our love for others as Saint Clare did. Amen.

ON SUNDAY
During Mass, listen for times the Holy Spirit is mentioned in readings, hymns, and prayers. Talk about what you heard.

 ON THE WEB
BlestAreWe.com
RCLBLectionary.com
SaintsResource.com

Saint Clare (1193–1253)

Clare, a friend and follower of Francis of Assisi, came from a wealthy Italian family in Assisi. She joined Francis in living a life of poverty and simplicity. Francis helped Clare found a religious community of women known as the Poor Clares. The nuns live a contemplative life of work and prayer. Their mission is to pray for the Church and for the world.

Feast Day: August 11

Take Home

Scripture Background
In the Time of Jesus

The Prayer of Petition Requests made to God are called prayers of petition. Jesus speaks of praying for one's needs and for the healing of the sick. He speaks of praying for ourselves and for others. Within the prayer of petition, however, is the understanding that while these prayers are offered to God in faith and expectation—through Christ and the Holy Spirit—God's responses are based on his will and what is best for the kingdom.

Some of Jesus' teachings about prayers of petition can be found in Matthew 6:5–15 and 7:7–11.

Our Catholic Tradition **in Liturgy**

The Holy Spirit's Role in Liturgy Prayers to the Holy Spirit reveal the Spirit's role in the liturgical life of the Church. During the Eucharistic Prayer at Mass, we petition God to send the Holy Spirit as Sanctifier to change the bread and wine into the Body and Blood of Christ. We also ask that the Holy Spirit changes us so that we, too, become holy and united in the Body of Christ.

The principal prayers of the Sacraments reveal more about the Holy Spirit's role. In Baptism we pray to the Holy Spirit for new life. In Confirmation we ask the Spirit to be our helper and guide. In Penance and Reconciliation we ask the Holy Spirit, as Comforter, to forgive our sins. Through the Holy Spirit we are given the grace to lead Christian lives.

The Holy Spirit Helps Us Pray

Come, Holy Spirit, fill our hearts with your love.
Based on the Pentecost Sequence

Share

We all need teachers. Teachers help us learn new words. Teachers show us how to do new things.

ACTIVITY

Who taught you how to tie your shoelaces?

_____

- -

_____

Who taught you how to write your name?

_____

- -

_____

Who taught you about Jesus?

_____

- -

_____

Who else teaches us how to pray?

 # A Special Teacher

Jesus told his friends many stories about prayer. One time Jesus said that we should pray always.

"How can we do that?" people asked. "We will grow tired. We will run out of things to say."

Another time, Jesus explained that the Holy Spirit teaches us to pray. This Spirit helps us turn everything we say and do into a prayer. The Spirit helps us even when we feel like giving up.

"Never give up," Jesus said. "When you pray, keep asking God for what you need. Keep knocking at God's door until he answers. For everyone who asks receives. Everyone who seeks finds. And to everyone who knocks, the door is opened."

Based on Matthew 7:7–8

Ways the Holy Spirit Helps Us

The Holy Spirit teaches us to pray. He helps us pray for what we need. We call these prayers **petitions**. Even our kind acts can become prayers. Helping a person shows our love for God. Our kind act becomes a prayer.

Our Church Teaches

At Mass we pray to the Holy Spirit. We ask the Holy Spirit to help us listen to the Bible readings. The priest asks the Holy Spirit to change the bread and wine into the Body and Blood of Christ. At the end of Mass, we ask the Holy Spirit to help us share our love with others.

ACTIVITY Draw about something or someone you are praying for.

We Believe

The Holy Spirit helps us pray in many ways. Even the good things we do can become prayers.

Faith Words

petitions
Petitions are asking prayers. We ask God to give us the things we need.

In what ways does the Church honor the Holy Spirit?

The Holy Parade

Lucia and her grandfather are on the church steps. She hears joyful music from a band. Then she sees the marchers coming down the street.

The men and boys wear colorful shirts and vests. The women and girls wear long dresses. Each group carries a bright banner.

Lucia asks, "Why are they marching?"

"It is a holy parade, or procession," her grandfather replies. "Every year, we honor the Holy Spirit in a special way. At Mass today, we will thank God for the gift of the Holy Spirit."

Why are the people having a procession?

PEACE

ACTIVITY

Write a petition to the Holy Spirit.
Ask the Holy Spirit to help you.
Then sign your name.

Come, Holy Spirit,

_____

- -

fill me with _____ .

Help me to

_____

- -

_____

_____

- -

_____ .

My name is

_____

- -

_____ .

In what ways can
we celebrate the
Holy Spirit?

187

A Holy Spirit Procession

We can pray to the Holy Spirit with a procession. We can play music and march. Then we can pray our petitions.

Leader: Come, Holy Spirit.
We know you are always with us.
Please listen to our prayers.

(Children read their petitions from page 187.)

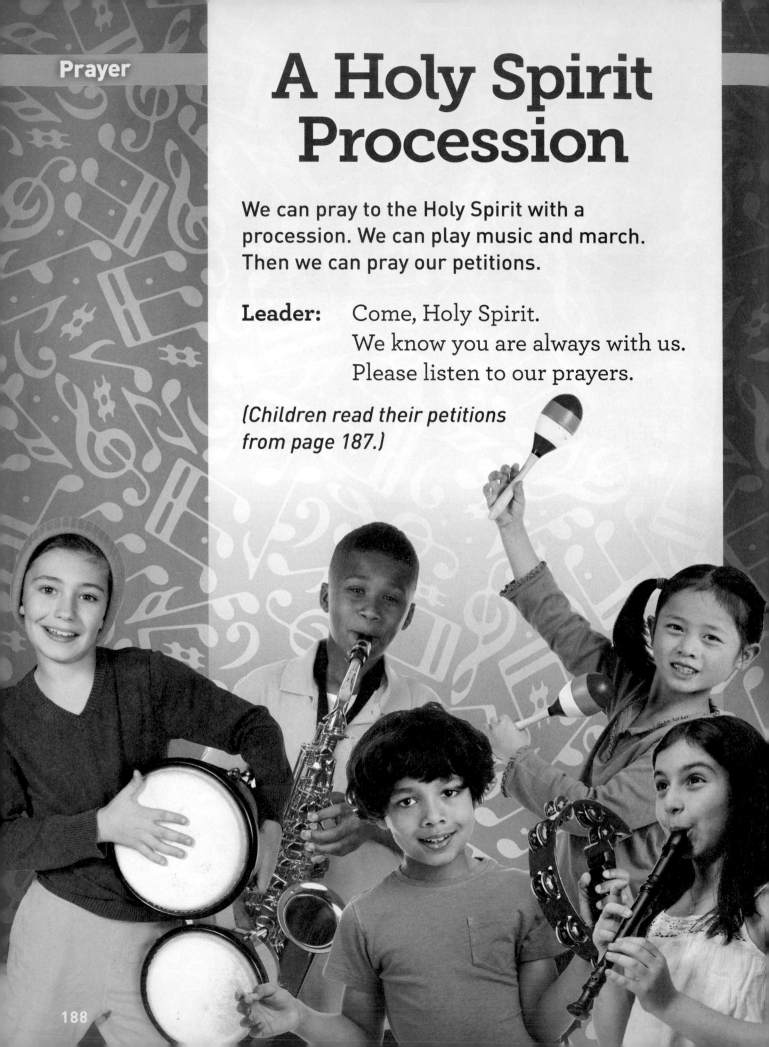

Chapter Review 16

A **Circle** the word that best completes each sentence.

1. Helping others can be a way to _____ .

    laugh   pray

2. Prayers that ask God for things we need are called _____ .

    petitions   praises

3. Jesus said that we should pray _____ .

    sometimes   always

4. The Holy Spirit teaches us to _____ .

    pray   play

B **Write** a petition to the Holy Spirit.

Come, Holy Spirit,
_____
- -
_____
_____
- -
_____ .

Faith in *Action*

Catechists Your religion teachers are sometimes called catechists. This is because they help form you in your faith. The Holy Spirit guides your catechist as Church and for the world. shares his or her faith.

In Your Parish

ACTIVITY You can ask the Holy Spirit to help your catechist. Color the border of the box. Then pray for your catechist.

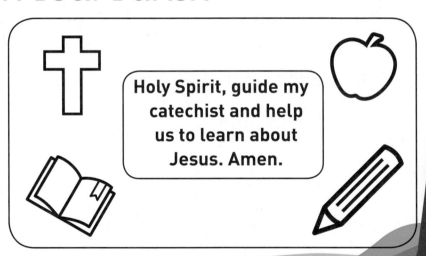

Holy Spirit, guide my catechist and help us to learn about Jesus. Amen.

In Everyday Life

ACTIVITY The Holy Spirit teaches us too! The Holy Spirit teaches us to pray. On each link of the chain, write the name of a person who needs prayers. Then pray for each person on your prayer chain.

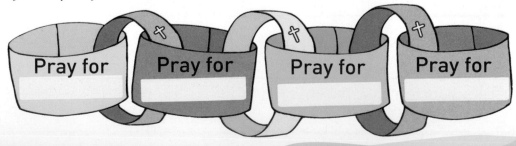

Pray for   Pray for   Pray for   Pray for

Jesus' Church of Followers

The Catholic Church throughout the world helps people in need. These people are our brothers and sisters. As baptized Christians, we are called to love and serve others.

... "Go into the whole world and proclaim the gospel to every creature."

Mark 16:15

Early Christians traveled this road to faraway countries. They helped people learn about Jesus. These children are helping by sending clothes to needy people around the world.

Laudate Dominum

Psalm 117, "Praise the Lord, all you peoples."

Music by Jacques Berthier

OSTINATO REFRAIN

Lau - da - te Do - mi-num, lau - da - te Do - mi - num

om - nes gen-tes, al - le - lu - ia. al - le - lu - ia.

Text: Taizé Community
Tune: Jacques Berthier
© 1980, Les Presses de Taize, GIA Publications, Inc., agent.

Followers of Jesus

The disciples were filled with joy and the holy Spirit.

Acts 13:52

Share

Our friends bring joy to our lives. We can do things with our friends. We can share things with our friends. We can tell our friends how we feel.

ACTIVITY

Draw something you do with a friend.

In what ways should Christians act?

🪔 The First Christians

After Christ rose from the dead, many people began to believe in him. They became his followers. Here is what these first Christians did.

The first Christians listened to the Apostles. They tried to live and act like Jesus. They prayed together and celebrated the Eucharist. They shared their food with each other. They helped people who were poor. They grew in faith and brought joy to one another.

Based on Acts 2:42–47

Acting as Christians

The followers of Jesus became the first members of the Church. They loved one another. Their **faith**, or belief in God, was strong. Jesus also calls us to be members of his Church. When we show love to others, we are true Christians.

Our Church Teaches

As Catholics, our faith helps us believe what our Church teaches. We say **"Amen"** to show that we believe. "Amen" is a prayer often prayed by the first Christians. We pray "Amen" many times at Mass. We pray "Amen" at the end of prayers we say each day. *Amen* means "Yes, I believe. It is true."

We Believe

Jesus invites us to belong to the Church. He wants our faith to be strong. Jesus wants us to love others.

Faith Words

faith
Faith is belief and trust in God.

Amen
Amen means "Yes, I believe. It is true." We often say "Amen" at the end of prayers.

ACTIVITY

Color the letters to show how you feel when you pray "Amen."

In what ways can we act like the first Christians?

197

Respond ## Saint Paul's Parish

The people of Saint Paul's parish try to act like the first Christians. Here are some ways they show love to others.

Mrs. Santos teaches children about Jesus.

Ava prays with others.

Vanessa takes care of young children.

There are six words in the Word Search.

The words tell what Christians should do.

Find the words and circle them.

listen ~~listen~~   ~~pray~~   ~~help~~

learn   talk   ~~share~~

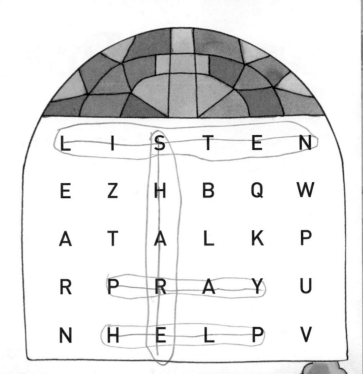

L I S T E N
E Z H B Q W
A T A L K P
R P R A Y U
N H E L P V

Ryan listens to a friend.

Mrs. Carr helps people who are poor.

Mr. Smith drives senior citizens to Mass on Sunday.

In what ways do we pray "Amen"?

A Prayer of Faith

"Amen" is a Christian prayer of faith. When we pray "Amen," we say yes to God. We say that we believe.

Let us pray "Amen" to what we believe.

Reader 1: Thank you, God, for the gift of the Church. We believe you want us to belong to the Catholic Church.

All: Amen.

Reader 2: Thank you, God, for the gift of creation. We believe you know us and care for us.

All: Amen.

Reader 3: Thank you, God, for the gift of Jesus. We believe he is your Son.

All: Amen.

Reader 4: Thank you, God, for the gift of the Holy Spirit. We believe your Spirit is always with us.

All: Amen.

A Draw a line to connect the parts of each sentence.

1. The first Christians tried to live and act   of the Church.

2. Belief and trust in God is called   like Jesus.

3. We end prayers with the word   faith.

4. Jesus' followers became the first members   Amen.

B Draw or write how you can act as a Christian.

Faith in Action

Christian Service Committee Many parishes have a Christian Service Committee. This group of helpers gives of their time and talent to serve those in need. They may collect food and clothing for the poor. They may comfort someone who is sick.

In Everyday Life

ACTIVITY A friend is sick. She has missed a week of school. She needs help. Think of one thing you could do to help her. Draw a picture to show how you would help.

do
shoing her hot to

In Your Parish

ACTIVITY Mr. Mann lost his job as a carpenter. His wife is ill and cannot work. Their children need clothes. How could your parish help?

We Celebrate Pentecost

Chapter 18

For the spirit of the LORD fills the world, . . .

Wisdom 1:7

Share

Birthdays are very special days.
Our families and friends celebrate with us.
They are glad that we belong to them.
When is your birthday?

_____

- -

_____

Month   Day

ACTIVITY

Circle the things that were part of your last birthday celebration.

Draw another special thing that was at your birthday celebration.

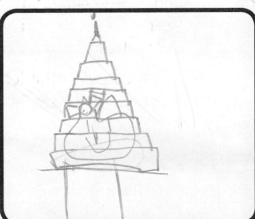

When does the Church celebrate her birthday?

205

Scripture

The Church's Birthday

When it was time for Pentecost, Jesus' followers were praying together. Suddenly there was a sound like a great wind blowing. The noise filled the whole house. Then flames, like tongues of fire, appeared over each person's head. The Holy Spirit filled all the people in the house with God's love. The Apostles and the others rushed outside. They began telling everyone about Jesus.

Outside there were people from many countries. These people spoke different languages. But they all understood what Jesus' followers were saying.

Based on Acts 2:1–6

Pentecost Sunday

We celebrate the birthday of the Church on **Pentecost Sunday**. We remember how Jesus' followers were filled with the Holy Spirit. We remember that the Holy Spirit helped them teach people from many countries about Jesus.

Our Church Teaches

The Church welcomes people of all races, languages, and abilities. Today people all over the world belong to the Church. Catholics are one family that lives together in **peace**.

We Believe

On Pentecost, the Holy Spirit filled Jesus' followers with God's love. The Church that began on Pentecost is now all over the world.

Faith Words

Pentecost Sunday
On Pentecost Sunday we celebrate the coming of the Holy Spirit and the birthday of the Church.

In what ways do Catholics try to live with everyone?

207

The Special Sunday

Pentecost is a special Sunday in Sylvia's parish. The children are invited to walk in a procession. They carry flags from many countries. Sylvia carries a flag from Mexico. Her friend Ravi carries the flag of India. The flags remind everyone that the Church is made up of people from all over the world.

During Mass the people sing in different languages. After Mass everyone goes outside to eat foods and play games from different countries.

What did the people in Sylvia's parish celebrate on Pentecost?

1. Many different people make up the Church.
   Many colors make a beautiful picture.
   Use the code to color the picture.
   What do you see?

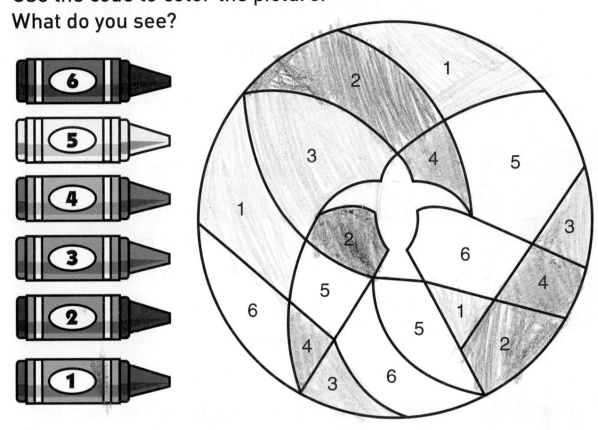

2. Circle the words that tell ways to keep peace.

   You are playing a game with a friend.

       cheat   play fair

   A friend calls you names.

       forgive   act mad

   There is one toy, but three people.

       take it   share it

   A family member needs you.

       help   watch TV

In what ways can
we celebrate the
Church's birthday?

A Quiet Prayer

Every day take time to be quiet and still. Think about where you have seen or felt Jesus and the Holy Spirit with you during the day.

Close your eyes and be quiet and still.

Listen carefully to your leader's words.

Leader: Remember that God is near.
Remember that God loves you.

Leader: Repeat after me in a quiet voice.
"Come, Lord Jesus . . .
Go away, worry! (*pause*)

"Come, Lord Jesus . . .
Go away, sadness!" (*pause*)

"Come, Lord Jesus . . .
Go away, trouble!" (*pause*)

Think about where you
saw Jesus today.
Where was the Holy Spirit?

Now be quiet and still again.
Feel God's love.
Know that God is near.

Based on Saint Ignatius' Jesus Prayer

Chapter Review 18

Complete the sentences with words from the box.

| Holy Spirit | Jesus | Pentecost Sunday | Apostles |

1. We celebrate the birthday of the Church on

   _Pe_ .

2. Pentecost celebrates the coming of the

   Hole Speret .

3. The Holy Spirit filled the followers of

   Jesuse with God's love.

4. The Holy Spirit helped the

   _P_ teach people of
   all countries about Jesus.

Faith in Action

Lectors   At Mass, we listen to readings from the Bible. The people who read the Word of God are called *lectors*. The lectors want us to hear God's message. They want us to believe the words we hear.

In Everyday Life

ACTIVITY   Choose a favorite Bible story from your book. Read the story to yourself. Then pretend you are a lector. Read the Word of God to others.

In Your Parish

ACTIVITY   On Pentecost, a lector reads aloud the Bible story about the coming of the Holy Spirit. Circle the words in the box that are in the Pentecost story. Then tell the story in your own words.

fifty days	praying	God's love
eating	Christmas	animals
Apostles	flames	Church
languages	Easter	born
Temple	wind	people
Jesus	children	water
Holy Spirit	followers	

The Church Helps the World

. . . "Go into the whole world and proclaim the gospel to every creature." Mark 16:15

Share

Before we can help others, we must find out what they need. Look at these pictures. What do the people need?

He needs

Medicine.

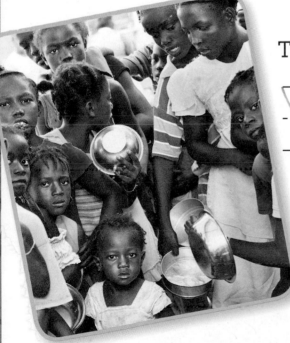

They need

Water.

She needs

a home.

Why should Christians help people in need?

215

🪔 The Need for Helpers

The Church of Jesus' followers grew quickly. There was too much work for the Apostles to do by themselves. So they asked the community to choose helpers. Some of these helpers were Stephen, Philip, and Nicholas. Stephen was good at telling people about God's Word in the Bible. The others made sure the people had food, clothes, and a place to live.

Then the Apostles had time to tell more people about Jesus. They had more time to lead people in prayer and to spread the Word of God.

Based on Acts 6:1–7

Christian Service

The first Christians learned that God calls everyone to help and **serve** others. They took care of their community. Helping people is our **mission**, too. When we take care of the needs of others, we follow Jesus.

Our Church Teaches

All the people in the world are our brothers and sisters. Many people need help. Each baptized person is called to love and serve others. The Holy Spirit helps us serve others with love, peace, and joy.

Faith Words

mission
Our mission as Christians is to love and serve others.

In what ways does the Church help people in need?

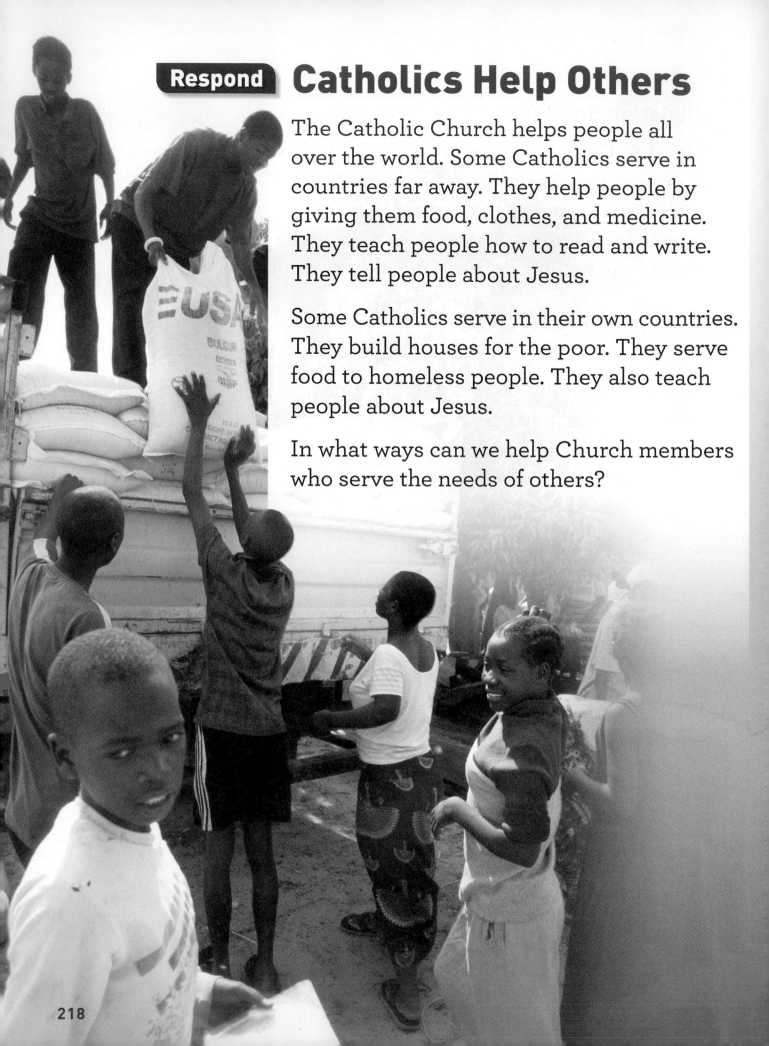

Catholics Help Others

The Catholic Church helps people all over the world. Some Catholics serve in countries far away. They help people by giving them food, clothes, and medicine. They teach people how to read and write. They tell people about Jesus.

Some Catholics serve in their own countries. They build houses for the poor. They serve food to homeless people. They also teach people about Jesus.

In what ways can we help Church members who serve the needs of others?

1. Draw one way you can help someone in need.

2. Write a prayer for church helpers who serve the needs of others.

_____

- -

_____

- -

_____

- -

_____

In what way can we get ready to be God's helpers?

Saying Yes to God

Leader: As you grow up, God asks you to love and serve others. Are you listening? Are you ready to say yes to God?

Let us pray about saying yes to God.

All: **God, our Creator, you called us by name to belong to your Church. As we grow up, help us to hear your voice. Give us the courage to say yes to your call. Amen.**

A **Circle** the words that best complete the sentences.

1. God calls everyone to _____ others.

   serve   hurt

2. We believe that _____ in the world are our brothers and sisters.

   some people   all people

3. As Christians, our _____ is to help others.

   mission   nation

4. The Holy Spirit helps us serve others with _____.

   candy and toys   love and joy

B **Draw or write** about how a Catholic today can answer God's call to serve others.

Faith in *Action*

Rosary for Peace Catholics all over the world pray the Rosary. They may say the Rosary for a special intention. Many say the Rosary as a prayer for peace in the world.

In Everyday Life

ACTIVITY Write or draw about a way you can be a peacemaker in your family, school, or neighborhood.

In Your Parish

ACTIVITY At Sunday Mass, your parish prays for peace in the world. Think of a place that needs peace. Make up your own prayer for peace. Share your prayer with a partner or with your religion class.

Take Home

We Pray with Holy Songs

By incorporating music into our prayer, we add a new dimension to the way we relate to God. This chapter encourages the children to think of Church music as an integral part of our worship experience. They will discover that hymns are prayers, and that when we sing with our hearts as well as our voices, we pray twice.

ACTIVITY **Feel the Music**

Play a song that your child likes. Have fun listening to the music and singing the words. Dance to the music with your child, expressing how the song makes you feel.

THROUGH THE WEEK

✝ **A PRAYER FOR THE WEEK** Dear God, we thank you for the gift of music. It comforts us when we feel sad and helps us express our joy. Help us lift our hearts and minds to you in song. Amen.

ON SUNDAY
During Mass, listen carefully to the words of the hymns. After Mass, discuss how they relate to the Scripture readings.

 ON THE WEB
BlestAreWe.com
RCLBLectionary.com
SaintsResource.com

Saint Cecilia (2nd century)

According to legend, Cecilia lived in Rome at a time of great persecution. At her wedding she sang hymns in her heart. Cecilia was responsible for the conversion of her pagan husband and his brother. All three were martyred. Cecilia is often pictured playing a harp or an organ. Many church choirs bear her name.

Patron Saint of: musicians
Feast Day: November 22

Take Home

♪ Scripture Background
Before the Time of Jesus and in the Early Church

Musical Instruments The most frequently mentioned biblical instrument is the *shofar*, or ram's horn, which is still used in synagogues today. In the Old Testament the *kinnor*, or David's harp, was actually a lyre used to accompany the praying of the psalms. Instruments mentioned in the New Testament include the harp, the flute, the lyre, the trumpet, and cymbals. The "resounding gong" referred to by Paul in 1 Corinthians 13:1 were actually vases set up to amplify actors' voices in Greek theaters.

You can read about the importance of religious music to the first Christians in Ephesians 5:18–20.

Our Catholic Tradition **in Music**

Spirituals Most African slaves in our country were not allowed to learn how to read or write. Many slaves were converted to Christianity. One way they kept their faith alive was by singing spirituals. These songs, based on Scripture, sustained the slaves in the same way the psalms sustained the Israelites during their captivity. The spirituals also helped slaves pass on their faith. Spirituals are now considered an art form as well as one of the original forms of music on this continent. As African Americans became Catholics, they brought with them their rich heritage in these biblically based hymns.

We Pray with Holy Songs

My heart is full of joy. I sing praises to my God.

Based on Psalm 28:7

Share

People sing for many reasons.

Songs put babies to sleep.

Songs remind us of our country.

Songs take away our fears.

Songs celebrate happy times.

ACTIVITY

What is your favorite song?

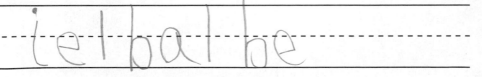

tel bal be

Why do
Christians sing?

225

Songs of the First Christians

When the first Christians celebrated the Eucharist, they did several things. They read the Bible. They prayed. They received the Body and Blood of Jesus. And they sang songs.

Why did they sing? Here is what Paul told the first Christians.

Be filled with God's Spirit. Sing psalms and hymns to God the Father. Sing your thanks and praise to God in the name of our Lord Jesus Christ.

Based on Ephesians 5:19–20

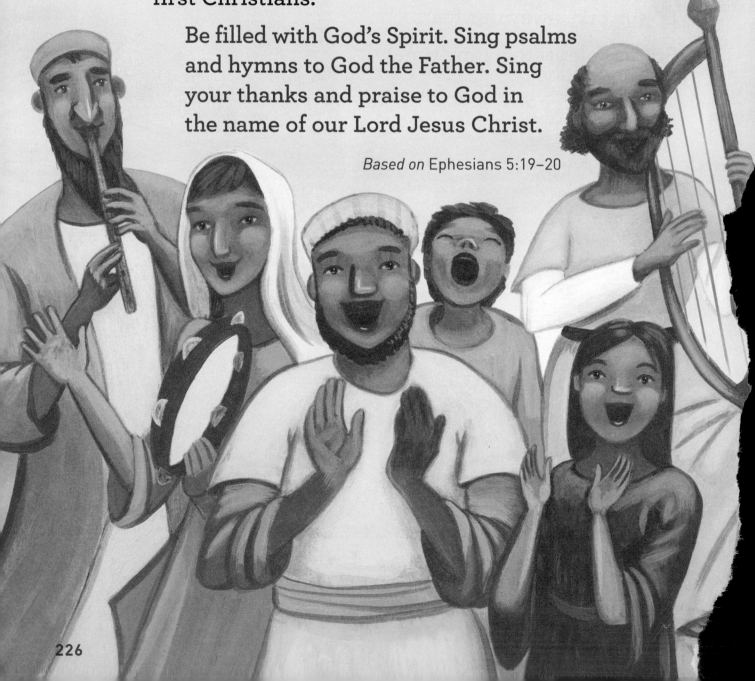

Praying with Holy Songs

The first Christians sang because the Holy Spirit filled them with joy. Singing **hymns**, or holy songs, helped them pray.

Saint Augustine said that when we sing to God, we pray twice. We pray with our voices and we pray with our hearts.

Our Church Teaches

We sing hymns at Mass to praise and thank God. Many of the words we sing come from the psalms and stories in the Bible. These holy songs help lift our hearts to God.

ACTIVITY

Add to the drawing on the page. Draw your family giving thanks and praise to God.

In what ways can we sing our thanks and praise to God?

227

Respond

Amanda Loves to Sing

Amanda loves to sing in the children's choir at her church. She sings as her parish community gathers to praise God. After the first Bible reading, she sings a psalm. She sings a hymn when people bring the bread and wine to the altar. She prays to God our Father when she sings the Lord's Prayer. Amanda sings at Communion time. She also sings at the end of Mass.

Sometimes during the week, Amanda hums or sings the songs from Mass. The music reminds her to give God thanks and praise. It reminds her to live in peace. It helps her love and serve others.

What holy songs do you like to hum or sing?

ACTIVITY

Use these words to complete the sentences.
Then write the words in the puzzle.

hymn   praise   pray   psalm   thanks

DOWN

1. We give God

3. Singing is a

way to _Pray_.

ACROSS

2. By singing, we

_____ _____ _____ _____ _____

_____ _____ _____ _____ _____ God.

_____ _____ _____ _____

3. A _____ _____ _____ _____ _____ is a song that is
also a prayer.

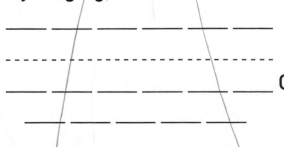

4. A  is a holy song.

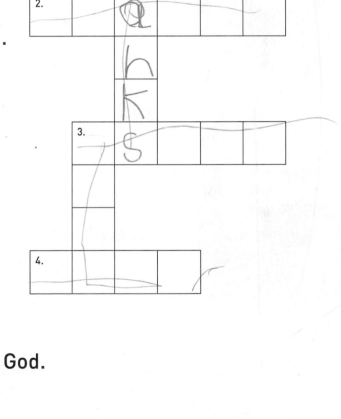

In what ways can
we celebrate our
good year?

A Song of Praise and Thanks

Leader: Our year together is coming to an end. Let us remember the good times we had. Let us sing our praise and thanks to God.

Side 1: Sing praise to God, everyone.

Side 2: Give thanks to God's holy name.

Side 1: Sing joyfully to God, and play music.

Side 2: With trumpets and horns, sing praise.

Based on Psalm 30:5 and Psalm 98:4–6

Leader: We thank you, O God, for a wonderful year. We thank you especially for *(each child names one thing)*.

Leader: Go now and share the Good News of Jesus with others.

All: **Thanks be to God.**

Chapter Review 20

A **Draw a line** to the word that best completes each sentence.

1. Holy songs are called

2. When we sing, we pray

3. Catholics sing hymns at

4. Hymns give God thanks and

praise.

hymns.

twice.

Mass.

B **Circle** the word that best completes each sentence.

1. Paul told the first Christians to sing ____ to God.

   ⬭stories⬭   psalms

2. The first Christians sang because the Holy Spirit filled them with ____.

   ⬭sorrow⬭   joy

3. Hymns can lift our ____ to God.

   ⬭hearts⬭   hands

4. Holy songs can remind us to live in ____.

   fear   peace

Faith in *Action*

Music Director   The music director chooses hymns to go with the Bible readings at Mass. She or he helps us learn new songs. The music director invites us to sing our praise to God.

In Everyday Life

ACTIVITY   Think about your favorite hymn, or holy song. Very quietly, sing the words to yourself. Tell a partner how this song can help you pray.

In Your Parish

ACTIVITY   Write a thank-you note to the music director in your parish. Share with him or her some of your favorite hymns and how you feel about singing those hymns at Mass.

Thank you!

Feasts and Seasons

The calendar of the Catholic Church is made up of special seasons. The weeks of each season celebrate the life and teachings of Jesus Christ.

Holy Week begins on Palm Sunday. It ends with three holy days. They remind us of the Last Supper, and that Jesus died and rose to new life to save all people.

HOLY WEEK

The Church year begins.

ADVENT
Our Church year begins on the first Sunday of **Advent**. We have four weeks to get ready to celebrate Jesus' birthday on Christmas.

ORDINARY TIME
In the second part of **Ordinary Time**, we learn more about the life and teachings of Jesus.

EASTER
The **Easter** season is a time of great joy. It begins on Easter Sunday. The Easter season lasts for fifty days. We celebrate that Jesus was raised from the dead. We sing, "Alleluia!"

LENT
The season of **Lent** lasts forty days. During Lent we get ready for Easter. We pray, give up things, and share what we have with others.

ORDINARY TIME
In the first part of **Ordinary Time** we learn how Jesus began his work among the people.

CHRISTMAS
During the **Christmas** season we celebrate that Jesus, the Son of God, came to Earth as our Savior.

Why Sunday is a Holy Day

Our Church celebrates Sunday as the most special day of the week. Catholics go to Mass on Sunday. At Mass we remember that Jesus died to save us. We remember that he was raised from the dead on Easter Sunday. That is why Sunday is called the Lord's Day.

Some very important holy days are celebrated on Sunday. We remember special times in Jesus' life. We honor Mary as the Mother of God. We celebrate the coming of the Holy Spirit.

Because Sunday is the Lord's Day, we also take time to relax. We spend time with our family and friends. We try to be helpful and kind.

Ordinary Time

 Love God, and love others as you love yourself.

Based on Luke 10:27

Colors of the Church Year

Each time a priest celebrates Mass, he puts on clothes called *vestments*. One of the vestments is called a chasuble. It looks like a beautiful poncho. The color of the chasuble changes with each season of the Church year.

Purple or violet is for Advent and Lent. White or gold is for Christmas and Easter. Red is for special days like Palm Sunday, Good Friday, and Pentecost Sunday. Green is for the weeks of Ordinary Time.

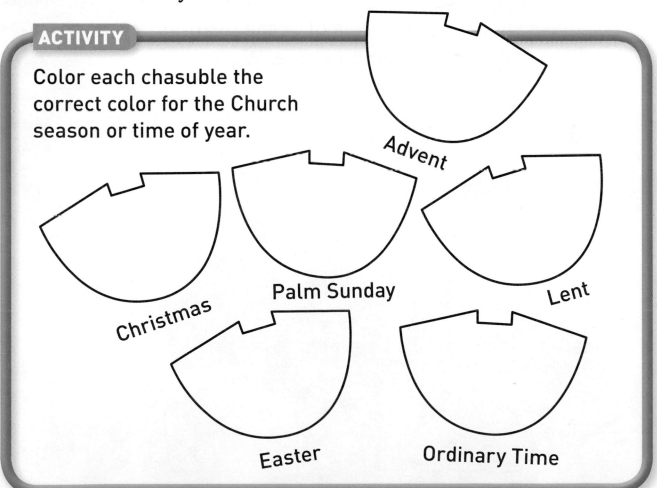

ACTIVITY

Color each chasuble the correct color for the Church season or time of year.

Advent

Christmas

Palm Sunday

Lent

Easter

Ordinary Time

A Time to Learn

Dear God, thank you for the Gospel stories that teach us about Jesus. Help us to follow him each day. Amen.

Ordinary Time is the longest part of the Church year. Most weeks of Ordinary Time are in the summer and fall. The Sundays are counted in order. For example, we say the Second Sunday in Ordinary Time. There are over thirty Sundays in Ordinary Time each year.

The Gospel readings during Ordinary Time are about the life and teachings of Jesus. At Mass we listen to stories of Jesus healing, blessing, and forgiving people. We learn ways to follow Jesus.

The Holy Guardian Angels

 I am sending an angel before you to guard you on the way. *Based on* Exodus 23:20

People Who Guard Us

Our families care for us. They try to keep us safe. Sometimes we need other people to guard us and guide us.

Look at the pictures and tell about the guards you see.

ACTIVITY

Draw a picture showing someone who guards you helping to keep you safe.

A Special Gift from God

Guardian angel, you are a gift from God. Thank you for watching over me. Amen.

God gives every person a guardian angel.

Guardian angels protect us and guide us.

They try to keep us from harm.

You can pray to your guardian angel. You can ask your angel to help you make good choices. You can pray that your angel will help you do what God wants. God puts you in the care of your guardian angel. Pray the prayer to your guardian angel on page 13. We celebrate the Feast of the Holy Guardian Angels on October 2.

Advent

 Get ready to welcome the Lord!

Based on Isaiah 40:3

Welcome to Our Home!

Sometimes we welcome guests to our homes. We want our guests to be happy. We get ready to welcome them in special ways. A friendly welcome makes our guests feel special.

ACTIVITY

Circle the pictures that show some of the ways your family welcomes guests.

A Time to Get Ready

Jesus, help me get ready to welcome you. Amen.

During **Advent** we get ready to welcome Jesus. We prepare our hearts. We do things for each other to show we care.

These are some of the ways our Church prepares us to welcome Jesus.

Each Sunday we light another candle on the Advent wreath.

We read Bible stories about people who waited for Jesus.

We care for those in need.

Saint Nicholas

 Be my follower by helping others.

Based on Matthew 19:21

Sharing

When you were a baby, you did not know how to share. Now you are older. You know it is important to share what you have with others.

Jesus Asks Us to Share

Even when it is hard, Jesus asks us to share what we have with others. Saint Nicholas did what Jesus asks. His story is on the next page.

ACTIVITY Is it easy to share it with others?

Circle your answer.   **Yes**   **No**

Read the word on each box. Does the word name something that you share with others? If it does, color the ribbon.

Bishop Nicholas

Saint Nicholas, you were a kind and loving person. Help us gladly share with others. Amen.

Nicholas was a bishop. In his work, he saw many poor children. Nicholas wanted to find ways to share what he had with them.

At night, when everyone was asleep, Bishop Nicholas went to the homes of the poor children. He left gifts of fruit, candy, and money on their doorsteps. Then he slipped quietly away. He did not want to be noticed!

Bishop Nicholas was a follower of Jesus. Nicholas shared what he had with those who had very little. Saint Nicholas is the patron saint of children. We celebrate the Feast of Saint Nicholas on December 6.

The angel said, "I have come from God to bring you good news of great joy."

Based on Luke 2:10

A Promise

"Guess what? My big brother promised to play soccer with all of us," said Sammy.

Sammy is very excited. He wants his brother to keep his promise.

ACTIVITY

Draw a picture about a promise that you made to someone.

God Keeps a Promise

God our Father, thank you for keeping your promise and sending Jesus to be with us. Amen.

On **Christmas**, we gather at Mass. We listen carefully to the Gospel story of Jesus' birth.

Some shepherds were watching their sheep near Bethlehem. An angel sent by God appeared and said, "Do not be afraid. I have come from God to bring you good news. God has kept his promise. Today the Savior has been born. You will find him lying in a manger."

Then angels in the sky sang out, "Glory to God in the highest." The shepherds ran and found Mary and Joseph and the baby Jesus. The shepherds praised God for all they had seen.

Based on Luke 2:8–20

The Holy Family

 Happy are you who love God and walk in his ways.   *Based on* Psalm 128:1

What Does Holy Mean?

Do you know what it means to be holy?
To be holy means to be like God.

What is God like?

God is full of love. God brings peace. God is kind and gentle. God cares for us. God forgives us.

ACTIVITY

The pictures tell what families do to become holy.

Color the words.

HELP

PRAY

CARE

Jesus' Family

Holy Family, help me be kind and loving to each person in my family. Amen.

The family of Jesus is called the Holy Family.

Mary is Jesus' mother. Joseph is Mary's husband and Jesus' foster father. Jesus loved and obeyed Mary and Joseph. They were kind and caring to Jesus and each other.

Feast of the Holy Family

During the Christmas Season, we celebrate the Feast of the Holy Family of Jesus, Mary and Joseph.

We celebrate the love that the members of the Holy Family have for each other. We honor God's love for all families.

Mary, the Holy Mother of God

 Hail, Mary!
You are full of God's grace.

Based on Luke 1:28

Mary Cares for Jesus

Look carefully at the pictures on this page.

Each picture shows ways that Mary cared for her Son, Jesus.

ACTIVITY

Circle the picture of Mary caring for Jesus that you like best.

Tell why you like the picture.

God Chose Mary

Mary, you are Mother of God and our mother too. Help us to grow in our love for your Son, Jesus. Amen.

God chose Mary to be the mother of his Son, Jesus. We call Mary the Mother of God. Mary is very special.

Mary cared for Jesus. Jesus wants Mary to love and care for us, too. He gave her to us as our special Mother. She loves us and cares for us. Mary prays for us. She tells Jesus about our needs.

We celebrate the Solemnity of Mary, the Holy Mother of God, on January 1.

Lent: Followers of Jesus

 "Follow me."

John 1:43

Followers of Jesus

Every day we try to become more like Jesus.
We are followers of Jesus. Jesus calls us to live
as he showed us. Jesus calls us to love
and care for each other.

ACTIVITY

You are a follower of Jesus.
Draw yourself in the picture
with other followers of Jesus.

Forty Days

*Jesus,
I want to be
more like you.
Help me to
be kind and
forgiving.
Amen.*

Lent lasts for forty days. During these forty days, we get ready to celebrate Easter. We try to become more like Jesus.

What Can We Do?

There are many things we can do during Lent to become more like Jesus. We can do some things with our parish community. We can do other things by ourselves.

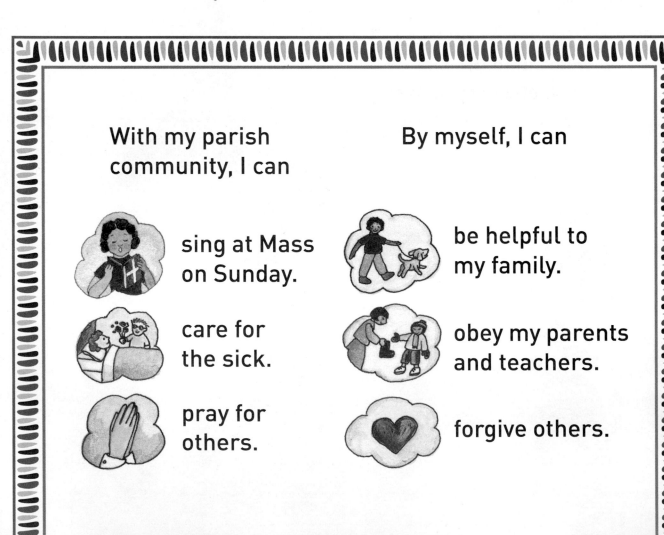

With my parish community, I can

sing at Mass on Sunday.

care for the sick.

pray for others.

By myself, I can

be helpful to my family.

obey my parents and teachers.

forgive others.

Lent: God's Promises

 I came to give you new life that will last forever. *Based on* John 10:28

New Life

Jesus promises his followers the gift of new life. At Baptism, we become members of the Church. The holy water of Baptism is a sign of our new life in Jesus. Many people prepare for Baptism during Lent.

ACTIVITY

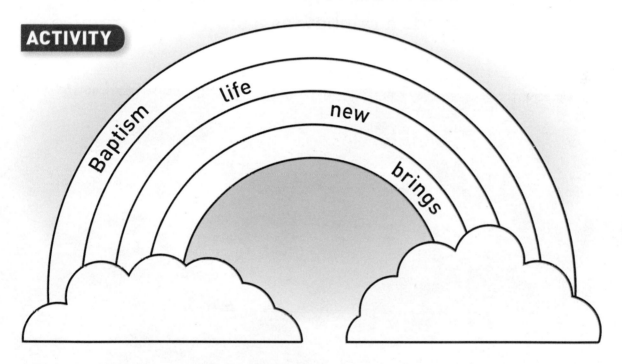

Use the words in the rainbow to write a sentence about Baptism. Then color the rainbow.

_____

- -

_____

- -

_____

God's Promise

Loving God, thank you for the gift of Baptism. I promise to follow Jesus always. Amen.

The Bible tells a story about Noah and a big flood. In the story, God sends water to flood the earth. Rain pours down for forty days. The rain almost washes everything away.

God saves Noah and his family from the flood. When the waters dry up, God makes a promise. God says that he will never let a flood destroy the earth again. Then God sends a rainbow as a sign of his promise.

Holy Week

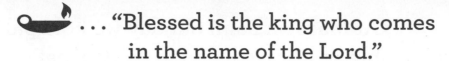 . . . "Blessed is the king who comes
in the name of the Lord."

Luke 19:38

Palm Sunday

The first day of Holy Week is called Palm Sunday. It is the Sunday before Easter. We remember how Jesus came into Jerusalem. His followers welcomed him with joy.

ACTIVITY

Read the story below.
Use the pictures to help you.

Palms are branches of .

Palm trees grow in hot, places.

One day a crowd of cheered and waved palms.

The people were happy to see .

They had a great parade to honor Jesus.

Palm Sunday Mass

Lord Jesus, we shout "Hosanna!" We welcome you as our King. Amen.

At Mass on Palm Sunday we hold palm branches. We listen to the Gospel story about Jesus going into the city of Jerusalem. We hear how the joyful crowd welcomed Jesus by shouting "Hosanna!"

We walk into church with the priest and our parish community. Like the people of Jerusalem, we say,

> . . . "Blessed is the king who comes in the name of the Lord."
>
> Luke 19:38

After Mass, we take our palm branches home. We welcome Jesus into our hearts and homes.

Easter

 "I have seen the Lord."

Based on John 20:18

Signs of Spring

Imagine that it is Sunday afternoon. You are taking a walk with your family. The sun is shining. The breeze feels warm. The air smells fresh and clean. You see many signs of new life. You are very happy that spring is here.

ACTIVITY

Look at the picture. Circle the signs of new life that you see.

Jesus Is Alive!

Risen Jesus, help us share in your new life. Alleluia! Amen.

Jesus died on a cross. His followers were very sad. They felt scared and all alone. They missed Jesus very much. Three days later God raised Jesus from the dead. God gave Jesus the gift of new life. Jesus' friends were filled with joy. The Risen Jesus was with them again. They thanked God for raising Jesus to new life.

We Celebrate Easter

Easter is our greatest feast. We celebrate Jesus' new life. We believe that we will share new life with Jesus forever. On Easter Sunday we go to Mass. We sing joyful songs. We pray joyful prayers. We sing and say, "Alleluia!"

Our Catholic Heritage

What Catholics Believe

We can learn about our faith from the Bible and from the teachings of the Church.

About
The Bible

The Bible is a special book about God. Some parts of the Bible tell how God loves and cares for people. Other parts tell about Jesus and his followers.

God chose many people to write the Bible. We believe that the Bible is the Word of God.

You can learn more about the Bible on pages 17–21 and in Chapter 3.

About
The Trinity

We believe there is only one God. We believe there is One God in Three Persons. The Three Persons are God the Father, God the Son, and God the Holy Spirit. We call the Three Persons the **Holy Trinity**.

We Believe in God the Father

God the Father created the world. He created all of us. Everything God made shows his love.

We are God's children. Like a loving father, God watches over us. He wants us to take care of the world. God wants us to care for each other.

We Believe in God the Son

The Son of God the Father became man. His name is Jesus. He lived on Earth to teach us how to love God the Father and one another.

Jesus died on the Cross and rose from the dead. He saved us from sin. Jesus Christ is our Savior.

We Believe in God the Holy Spirit

The Holy Spirit is God. He is the gift of the love of God the Father and God the Son. The Holy Spirit is always with us.

The Holy Spirit gives us grace to help us follow Jesus. Grace is God's loving presence in our lives.

About

The Catholic Church

We belong to the Catholic Church. We are called Catholics. We are followers of Jesus.

The pope is the leader of the Catholic Church all over the world. He lives in Rome. We call the pope our Holy Father.

A bishop is the leader of a diocese. A diocese is made up of many parishes. A bishop teaches and cares for the people of his diocese. The pope and the bishops tell us what Catholics belive. Today the Apostles are with us through the pope and the bishops.

A priest serves the people of a parish. He celebrates Mass with the parish community. He teaches people about the Good News of Jesus. A priest needs many helpers to care for all the people in the parish.

chalice —

paten   crucifix   candle

About
A Visit to Church

A Catholic church is a very special place to visit.

We go to church to worship God. We go to church to celebrate Mass with our parish community.

Look at the pictures. They show some things that we can see in our parish church.

presider's chair

altar

tabernacle

sanctuary lamp

ambo

About
Mary

Mary was good and holy. God chose her to be the mother of his Son, Jesus. Mary loved and trusted God. She loved and cared for Jesus.

Mary is our Mother, too. Like a good mother, Mary loves and cares for us.

Mary is our greatest **saint**. We honor Mary by calling her Mother of God. We ask Mary, the Mother of God, to pray for us.

About
New Life Forever

Jesus teaches us how to love God and others. Jesus says that if we act with love, we will have new life. Jesus promises that if we love God and others, we will live forever.

When we die we will be with Jesus, Mary, and all the good and holy people who ever lived. Happiness with God forever is called **Heaven**.

How Catholics Worship

Worship is giving honor and praise to God. We worship when we pray and when we celebrate the Sacraments.

About
The Sacraments

The Sacraments are celebrations of God's love for us. We celebrate that we are followers of Jesus Christ. We celebrate that we share in his new life.

Baptism is the Sacrament of welcome into the Church. At Baptism we become children of God. The water of Baptism washes away all sin and fills us with God's grace.

Confirmation is the Sacrament in which the Holy Spirit makes our faith in Christ stronger. The Holy Spirit helps us share the Good News of Jesus.

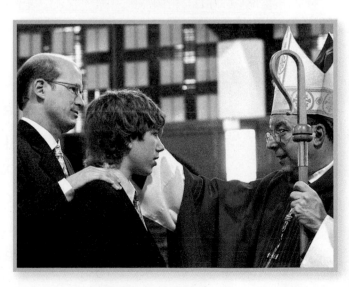

The **Eucharist** is the Sacrament in which Jesus Christ shares himself with us. We receive the Body and Blood of Christ.

Penance and Reconciliation is the Sacrament of forgiveness. We say that we are sorry for our sins. We celebrate God's forgiveness.

Anointing of the Sick is the Sacrament that brings the peace of Jesus to people who are sick.

Holy Orders is the Sacrament that celebrates the mission of deacons, priests, and bishops. These men are called to serve God's people in a special way.

Matrimony is the Sacrament that celebrates the love of a baptized man and a baptized woman for each other. They promise to be faithful to each other their whole life. They are ready to begin their family life.

About
The Mass

1. Our celebration begins. We stand and sing a welcome song. The priest and other ministers go to the altar.

2. We make the Sign of the Cross. The priest welcomes us with these words: "The Lord be with you."

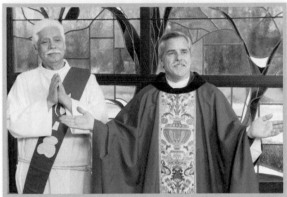

3. We remember our sins. We ask God to forgive us.

4. We listen to the Word of God in readings from the Bible. After each of the first two readings we say, "Thanks be to God."

5. The priest or deacon reads the Gospel. The word *gospel* means "good news." We stand and listen to the Good News of Jesus. We say, "Praise to you, Lord Jesus Christ."

6. The priest or deacon helps us understand Jesus' message in a special talk called the homily.

7. In the Prayer of the Faithful, we ask God to help the Church, our country, and all of God's people.

8. We bring the gifts of bread and wine to the altar for the holy meal with Jesus. We remember that Jesus always loves us.

9. The priest blesses God and offers him our gifts of bread and wine. We say, "Blessed be God for ever."

10. We thank and praise God for all of our blessings. We especially thank God for the gift of Jesus.

11. The priest prays as Jesus did at the Last Supper. Our gifts of bread and wine become the Body and Blood of Jesus Christ.

12. The priest holds up the Body and Blood of Jesus. He says a prayer to praise God. We answer, "Amen."

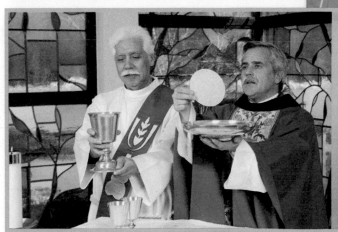

13. We say the Lord's Prayer. This is the prayer that Jesus taught us to say.

14. We offer one another a Sign of Peace. This is a sign that reminds us to live as Jesus teaches us to live.

15. We receive Jesus in the Eucharist. Sharing Jesus' Body and Blood in a special way means that we are promising to follow Jesus.

16. We receive God's blessing. We answer, "Amen." We sing a song of praise. We go in peace to love and serve God and one another.

How Catholics Live

Jesus teaches us how to live. He gives us the Holy Spirit and the Church to help us.

About
The Great Commandment

God's laws are really one Great Commandment. Jesus said, "You must love God above all things and love your neighbor as yourself" (based on Mark 12:30–31). The Great Commandment tells us how to love God and other people.

About
The New Commandment

Jesus gave us a New Commandment. He said, "Love one another as I have loved you" (based on John 13:34). We show our love for others when we are helpful and kind.

About
The Ten Commandments

The Ten Commandments are God's laws, or rules, that tell us how to show our love for God, ourselves, and other people.

God's Laws	We Live God's Laws
1. I am the Lord your God: you shall not have strange gods before me.	We believe in God and love God.
2. You shall not take the name of the Lord your God in vain.	We use God's name with love.
3. Remember to keep holy the Lord's day.	We celebrate Mass with our parish community. We keep the Lord's Day holy.
4. Honor your father and your mother.	We obey our parents and those who care for us.
5. You shall not kill.	We care for all living things.
6. You shall not commit adultery.	We respect our bodies and the bodies of others.
7. You shall not steal.	We respect what is given to us and what belongs to others.
8. You shall not bear false witness against your neighbor.	We always tell the truth.
9. You shall not covet your neighbor's wife.	We rejoice in the happiness of others.
10. You shall not covet your neighbor's goods.	We do not want more than we need.

Based on Exodus 20:2–17

About
Sin and Forgiveness

Sin is a choice to do something that we know is wrong. Sin is turning away from God. Sin hurts our friendship with people.

We know that God loves us. We know that he is always ready to forgive us. God wants us to be sorry for our sins. He wants us to promise to do better. We can ask the Holy Spirit to help us.

Dear God,

I am sorry for what I did wrong. I will try to do better. I will love and care for others. Please send the Holy Spirit to help me.

Amen.

Jesus teaches us to love and care for others. Sometimes people do wrong things to us. We should always be ready to forgive them. We can say, "I forgive you."

About
Vocations

We become members of the Catholic Church at Baptism. God calls us to love him and serve him in a special way. This is called our *vocation*.

Religious Vocations

God calls some people to a special life of service in the Church. The call to be a priest, deacon, and religious sister or brother is called a *religious vocation*.

Many priests serve the Church by being leaders of parish communities. Others teach or work with poor people.

Deacons help the priests in parishes. They lead celebrations of Baptism and Marriage. At Mass, they teach people about the Bible readings. Deacons visit the sick and pray with families of people who have died.

Many religious sisters and brothers serve in parishes. They make holy promises called *vows*. The vows help them put Jesus first in their lives. They share the Good News of Jesus.

Other Calls to Serve

God calls all Catholics to serve the Church. Some Catholics help at Mass. They welcome people. They read aloud from the Bible. They lead the singing of holy songs. They help give Holy Communion to the people.

Other Catholics teach children and adults about God's love. They share the Good News about Jesus. They teach people to pray in different ways.

Many Catholics visit the sick and help the poor. They give money to help people in need.

As you grow up, God will call you to serve the Church in special ways. Will you be ready to say "yes" to his call?

How Catholics Pray

Prayer is talking with and listening to God. We can pray anywhere and at any time. God is everywhere. God always hears our prayers.

About

Kinds of Prayer

There are many different ways to pray. We can say the prayers we learn at home, at school, and in church. We can use our own words to pray, too. Sometimes we can just be quiet in God's presence. We do not even have to say any words.

Our thoughts can be a prayer. Our hopes can be a prayer. This kind of prayer is called *meditation*. In meditation we use our imagination to think about God. We think about what God wants us to do.

We can use our bodies when we pray. When we make the Sign of the Cross, we use our hands. Sometimes we kneel when we pray. We can even sing or dance as a prayer to God.

We are never alone when we pray. God always hears our prayers.

About
The Lord's Prayer

The Lord's Prayer is a very special prayer. Jesus taught us the words. In this prayer, Jesus teaches us to call God "our Father." We believe that God is everyone's loving Father.

Our Father, who art in heaven, hallowed be thy name;

God is our Father. We praise God's holy name.

thy kingdom come,

We pray that everyone will know God's love and live in peace.

thy will be done on earth as it is in heaven.

We pray that everyone will follow God's law.

Give us this day our daily bread,

We pray for our needs and the needs of others.

and forgive us our trespasses, as we forgive those who trespass against us;

We ask God to forgive us when we sin.
We remember that we must forgive others.

and lead us not into temptation,

We ask God to help us make good choices.

but deliver us from evil.

We pray that God will protect us from harm.

Amen.

"Amen" means that we believe the words we say.

Write-in Glossary

Advent
(page 234)

_____

- -

_____ is the time before Christmas when we get ready to welcome Jesus into our lives.

Amen
(page 197)

_____

- -

_____ means "Yes, I believe. It is true." We often say "Amen" at the end of prayers.

angel
(page 113)

_____

- -

An _____ is a helper or a messenger from God.

Anointing of the Sick
(page 266)

_____   _____

-          - - - - - - - - - - - - - -

_____ of the _____ is the Sacrament that brings the peace of Christ to people who are sick.

Baptism
(page 81)

_____

- -

In _____ the Church welcomes us as new members. Baptism takes away our sins.

Bible
(page 49)

_____

- - - - - - - - - - - - - - - - - -

The _____ is the Word of God written by human writers. The Holy Spirit guided them.

Blessed Sacrament
(page 124)

_____ _____

The _____ _____ is another name for the Eucharist.

blessing
(page 42)

_____

A _____ is a gift from God. It can also be a prayer that asks for God's protection and care.

Catholic Church
(page 29)

_____ _____

The _____ _____ is the community of Jesus' followers to which we belong. The Church tells everyone about Jesus.

Christ
(page 123)

_____

_____ is another name for Jesus. It reminds us that Jesus was sent by God to save all people.

Christians
(page 175)

_____

_____ are people who love Jesus Christ and follow him.

Christmas
(page 235)

_____

_____ is when Jesus, the Son of God, came to Earth as our Savior.

_____

- -

church
(page 38)

A _____ is a special place where Catholics come together to pray.

_____

- -

community
(page 29)

A _____ is a group of people who belong together.

_____

- -

Confirmation
(page 165)

_____ is the Sacrament in which the Holy Spirit makes our faith in Jesus Christ stronger.

_____

- -

Creation
(page 71)

_____ is everything that God made.

_____

- -

Creator
(page 71)

God is our _____. God made everything in the world.

_____

- -

Eucharist
(page 123)

The _____ is the holy meal where Jesus' sacrifice on the Cross is made present again.

_____

- - - - - - - - - - - - - - - - - - -

faith
(page 197)

Our _____ is our belief and trust in God.

forgive
(page 133)

The word _____ means to excuse or to pardon.

Fruits of the Holy Spirit
(page 175)

The _____ of the _____

_____ are signs that the Holy Spirit is acting in our lives. Some fruits are love, joy, peace, patience, gentleness, kindness, and self-control.

Gloria
(page 60)

The _____ is a prayer of praise to God. It is often said or sung at Mass.

Gospel
(page 143)

The _____ is the Good News of Jesus. There are four Gospels in the Bible.

grace
(page 81)

The gift of _____ is God's life in us. It fills us with his love.

hallowed
(page 101)

The word _____ means holy.

Heaven
(page 91)

_____ is happiness with God forever.

holy
(page 91)

To be _____ means to be like God.

_____ _____

Holy Orders
(page 266)

_____ _____ celebrates the mission of deacons, priests, and bishops.

Holy Spirit
(page 155)

The _____ _____ is God. The Holy Spirit helps us follow Jesus.

Holy Trinity
(page 260)

The _____ _____ is One God in Three Persons—God the Father, God the Son, and God the Holy Spirit.

Hymns
(page 227)

_____ are holy songs that lift our hearts to God.

Jesus
(page 113)

_____ is the Son of God.

Last Supper
(page 123)

The _____ _____ is the special meal that Jesus shared with his friends on the night before he died.

Lord's Prayer
(page 101)

The _____ _____ _____ is the prayer that Jesus taught us.

Matrimony
(page 266)

The Sacrament of _____ celebrates the love that a baptized man and a baptized woman have for each other.

Mary
(page 113)

_____ is the mother of God's Son.

Mass
(page 38)

The holy meal that Jesus shares with us at _____ is called the Eucharist.

mercy
(page 136)

God's _____ is his loving forgiveness. We are called to show mercy to others.

mission
(page 217)

Our _____ as Christians is to love and serve others.

parish
(page 39)

A _____ is a group of Catholics who belong to the same church community.

Penance and Reconciliation
(page 266)

_____

- -

_____ and

_____

- -

_____ is the
Sacrament that celebrates God's forgiveness.

Pentecost Sunday
(page 207)

_____ _____

- -

_____ _____
celebrates the coming of the Holy Spirit and the
birthday of the Church.

Petitions
(page 185)

_____

- - - - - - - - - - - - - - - - - - - -

_____ are prayers asking God
to give us the things we need.

praise
(page 59)

_____

- - - - - - - - - - - - - - - - - - - -

A prayer of _____ celebrates
God's goodness.

Prayer
(page 59)

_____

- - - - - - - - - - - - - - - -

_____ is listening to and talking
to God.

Psalms
(page 143)

_____

- - - - - - - - - - - - - - - -

_____ are prayers from the Bible that
people often sing. The Book of Psalms is in the Bible.

Sacraments
(page 165)

The _____ are special signs of God's love.

saint
(page 264)

A _____ is a special person who lived a holy life. Mary is our greatest saint.

Savior
(page 113)

Our _____ is Jesus, the Son of God.

serve
(page 217)

To _____ means to help other people.

sin
(page 133)

To _____ is to choose to do something that we know is wrong. When we sin we turn away from God.

tabernacle
(page 123)

A _____ is a special place in church where the Blessed Sacrament is kept.

Temple
(page 142)

The _____ was a special building in Jerusalem. Jesus prayed in the Temple and learned about God.

Index

Credits